Thomas Davis

THE IRISH WRITERS SERIES
James F. Carens, General Editor

THOMAS DAVIS

Eileen Sullivan

Lewisburg
BUCKNELL UNIVERSITY PRESS
London: Associated University Presses

© 1978 by Associated University Presses, Inc.

Associated University Presses, Inc.
Cranbury, New Jersey 08512

Associated University Presses
Magdalen House
136-148 Tooley Street
London SE1 2TT, England

Library of Congress Cataloging in Publication Data

Sullivan, Eileen A.
  Thomas Davis.

  (Irish writers series)
  Bibliography: p.
  1. Davis, Thomas Osborne, 1814-1845—Criticism and
interpretation.
PR4525.D58Z86   821'.8   72-4182
ISBN 0-8387-1234-7
ISBN 0-8387-1237-1 pbk.

Printed in the United States of America

Contents

67565

Chronology

1814   Born October 14 at Mallow, County Cork.

1836   Graduated Trinity College, Dublin Law School.

1837   Published *The Reform of the Lords.*

1839   "The Utility of Debating Societies in Remedying the Defects of University Education," delivered to Trinity College Historical Society.

1840   "The Young Irishman of the Middle Classes," delivered to Trinity College Historical Society; appeared in *The Nation,* 1848.

1841   "Udalism and Feudalism," *Citizen.*

1842   October 15 joined Charles Gavan Duffy and John Blake Dillon to establish *The Nation.*

1842–1845 Literary, social, educational, and political essays; poems; ballads and songs written for *The Nation.*

1843   *The Patriot Parliament of 1689, with its Statutes, Votes, and Proceedings.*

1845   *John Philpot Curran.*

1845   Died September 16, Dublin. Buried in Mount Jerome Cemetery, Dublin.

Introduction

Thomas Davis, a nineteenth-century Irishman, is generally remembered as a journalist because he, with Charles Gavan Duffy and John Blake Dillon, established and co-edited *The Nation.* Their purpose was to identify, unify, and solidify the various factions of the national movement.

Davis was a journalist of an extraordinary nature, however, because of the literary quality of his national writings. These works revealed an ethnocentrism that rarely cited the vices, shortcomings, and biases of his people. For Davis, *The Nation* was a propagandistic medium through which he communicated his ideas about nationality. Moreover, because of his Protestant background and his sensitivity to the emerging Catholic nationalism initiated by Daniel O'Connell, Davis seldom criticized the Catholic population. Indeed, he acted as a catalyst to Catholic patriotism by giving direction and support to the nationalist feelings of Catholics. Writing to forge a nation that would include the Catholic majority, he also appealed to the imagination of the Protestant Ascendency. In the process he created a lasting collection of poems, songs, and essays that transcend the purpose for which they were written.

Today we may read the poems and listen to the songs and be moved to pity or joy because they evoke a human response to the suffering, sorrow, nobility of spirit, and neighborliness that Davis witnessed as he walked the Irish roads. Through his analytic prose works we are persuaded to agree with his conclusions about the Protestant role in leading the country toward a political entity. Over and over again Davis pointed out the responsibility of the educated class to correct the abuses of political power and social inequities.

Addressing himself to the majority, Davis wrote simply and traditionally to bring together an aroused rural and urban people. Addressing himself to the minority, he wrote complexly and legalistically to awaken the Protestant dreamer. Consequently, his writings fall into two distinct categories. There are the poems, songs, ballads, and essays in *The Nation,* which are part of the romantic nationalism that swept Europe during the nineteenth century. Davis, if in Italy, for instance, would have been a member of the Young Italy movement because, like Mazzini, the young Irishman wrote to evoke a nationalistic pride in language, literature, history, geography, morals, customs, traditions, and cultural values. Basically, Davis was a local-color writer describing in polychrome the dress, dialect, attitude, aspirations, fears, and frustrations of the Irish people through epithalamium, eulogy, and eponym. Then there are the nonfictional prose writings, *The Reform of the House of Lords* and *The Patriot Parliament* that resembled English political journalism of the day, in particular that of Thomas Carlyle. Davis adapted his style to focus national attention upon the current autocratic British political corruption in the House of Lords and the democratic structure of the past Irish Parliament of 1689. In *John Philpot Curran,* Davis recorded the life and work of an Irish lawyer dedicated to a fair interpretation of law.

Since Irish political action after the Catholic Emancipation Act of 1829 had slowed down and the aging O'Connell could not supply the energy to move the inert mass, Davis through his poetry and prose would energize the entire nation to activate the body politic. He sought to arouse the Catholics and the Protestants by writing from their perspectives. Davis, with a poet's soul, played the role of nation builder. He presupposed that a nation could be constructed from disparate elements because he believed in a universe in which order follows chaos. Poetic justice was basic to both his romantic nationalism and his political journalism. Davis's death in 1845, when he was only 31 years of age, deprived the national movement of a driving force and an invigorating intellect, but his thoughts inspired the revolutionaries of 1916.

Thomas Davis

1

Prose Works and Nationalism

When Thomas Davis was born in Mallow in 1814, Ireland had just passed through thirteen years of non-representative government. Since the "union" with the British Crown in 1801, Ireland had been ruled from Westminster. Ironically, the majority of the Anglo-Irish Protestant Ascendency, which Davis tried to arouse, had, along with the Roman Catholic Irish, no active political life. But inevitably, individuals from both classes combined their political energies in the pursuit of civil rights. Davis's early prose works — *The Reform of the Lords* (1837), "The Young Irishman of the Middle Classes" (1840), and "Udalism and Feudalism" (1841), — explain his joining Charles Gavan Duffy and John Blake Dillon, two Catholic Irishmen, in establishing *The Nation.*

Davis thought that political stability could be attained by changing the structure of the House of Lords, and he offered a solution to the diseased political system in *The Reform of the Lords,* a thirty-four page pamphlet published in Dublin under the nom de plume of "A Graduate of the Dublin University." He was then

twenty-three years old, just home from his last term as a
law student in London.

Convinced that a rational approach to the Irish
problem existed, Davis proves to his own satisfaction
that only a reform of the Peers will solve the difficulties.
He addresses himself to all factions but the unre-
claimable Orangemen. Recognizing the danger of the
unchecked political power of the Peers, Davis wants it
curtailed. He suggests that the Lords be elected from the
entire Peerage; the ballot would control the actions of
the House of Lords rather than their tie by kinship or
interest to the crown. "Routine elections, similar to
those in America, . . . would secure the ablest
assembly." The young graduate, dismissing the argument that the Peers are directly subject to God, states
that liberty can not exist so long as the House of Lords
exists. Corruption, bribery, and control over the Commons are dangerous attributes of the Upper House.
Hereditary rank must be abolished; rank should be
granted for service to the state. Duke or earl could then
stand for election and form a vital part of the government. Since there were 180 members in the House of
Lords, thirty should be elected each year; every sixth
year a Lord would stand for election and account for his
past actions. The thrust of Davis's argument is that a
representative, responsible House of Lords would "pur-
sue the interests of the nation."

These sentiments are also expressed in his address
"The Young Irishman of the Middle Classes," delivered
before the members of the College Historical Society of
which he was president. The Society, founded in 1839,
was composed of liberal and conservative students and

young university men. Most were Protestants, seeking political and literary fame. Davis warns them, though, that they will be facing opposition from the Irish Catholics, who represent seven-eighths of the nation but are barred from Trinity College because of their religion. Now, despite the "most preverse opposition chronicled in the annals of even our Anglo-Irish bigotry," middle-class Ireland was establishing provincial colleges. The graduates will compete with and compel the Protestant upper class to fight for political and literary laurels.

In the address before the Trinity group, Davis criticizes the educational curriculum at Trinity because it favors classical over modern knowledge. A student, he argues, should know Irish history and study current English, French, and German works instead of Greek and Roman works. Since man can not master all knowledge, let him know his own nature and duties, and the mores of his own society. Quite bluntly, Davis outlines the vices of the university system. Doubting that academic reform could correct the ills, he wants to build a new structure to provide knowledge of Irish natural and civil history, language, and literature.

From a religious point of view, the address rejects gloomy Calvinistic invective against the nature of man. Davis conceives of a joyous human nature created by God, and of man as using his errors for self-instruction. Most of the address, however, relates to the political distress of Ireland. Davis reminds his listeners that they are Irishmen who should consecrate all their energies to her cause. "The poor and the pest-houses are full," Davis says, "the valleys of her country and the streets of her metropolis swarm with the starving." In summing up, Davis tells his colleagues to seek "happiness, holiness, and peace." For his audience, he wishes all members successful, honorable careers that will render them "better fitted for eternity."

Charles Gavan Duffy in his *Short Life of Thomas Davis (1840-1846)* says that the address surprised Davis's friends as well as the bulk of the audience. It earned the respect and admiration of political opponents and excited the feelings of his friends. Actually, his public life began with this patriotic address, written from his personal observations of contemporary Ireland and from the perspective he held from 1840 until his death in 1845.

Shortly after this address to the members of the Historical Society, he began his career in journalism in an ecumenical environment. Davis contributed to the *Citizen,* managed by his Protestant friends McCullagh and Wallis, and to the *Morning Register,* a Whig Catholic paper, edited by John Blake Dillon.

Ironically, Davis appeals to Irish Protestant nationality in the *Morning Register* on February 2, 1841. Greatly angered by Dublin Castle's decision to cut the Parliamentary funds for the Royal Dublin Society — created by the Irish Parliament before the Union of 1801 to foster Irish arts and sciences — Davis defends a conservative Protestant institution in a Whig Catholic paper. Membership in the Royal Dublin Society was restricted to rich Protestants. When Dr. Murray, the Catholic Archbishop of Dublin, tried to join, he was refused membership. The Whig government, which Dr. Murray supported, voted to withdraw support shortly after the incident. Davis in his argument does not defend the exclusion of Dr. Murray; he denounces that decision. However, the young reformer points to the arbitrary role of the government in destroying a national institution. With fire in his eyes, he writes, "Would the French or English Governments treat a public institution thus? No, they dare not." Therefore the government should not destroy an Irish public institution that was over a hundred years old and had eight hundred members. The Society was saved, and Davis and Dillon eventually became good friends, announcing themselves followers of Daniel O'Connell. This declaration was a momentous one. For Davis, it meant moving from the idea of rights, duties, and responsibilities of citizenship as noted in *The Citizen* to the concept of nationality, as it would be expressed in *The Nation*.

In "Udalism and Feudalism," an article prepared for *The Citizen,* Davis tries to reach the educated Anglo-Irish Protestants, appealing to their sense of justice about the corrupt land system. He gathers his facts and forces the reader to make the same inferences. Davis believes that the greater the number of statistics, the greater the probability that his readers will share his conviction. He desperately desires them to share his conclusion: each man must own the land he farms. The future prosperity and political independence of Ireland, he asserts, is bound to that conclusion. Viewed in retrospect, he was quite right. The sociopolitical stability of Ireland and its economic prosperity depended upon a just land tenure in which labor and management shared the profits. Despite the crosscurrents of political and religious forces, the Irish mainstream had to include all tributaries before regaining its national stature in European cultural movements.

Davis, a spiritual father to Michael Davitt and James

Connolly, understood the source of Ireland's socio-
economic problems: absentee landlordism, which had a
stranglehold upon tenants, small farmers, and agricultural workers. In the two parts of "Udalism and
Feudalism" Davis outlines the horrors of such a land
system. From a historical point of view, he points out
the value of udalism in which the wants of the tribe or
nation determine the ownership of its territory and
inheritance of land through gavelkind (as opposed to
primogeniture). In all laws— the Indian, the Jewish, the
Greek, the Celtic, the Roman, the Persian, and the
Teutonic— Davis writes, subdivision among the family
was the custom until rules of conquest changed the
distribution of land and the life of its inhabitants. After
centuries of violence, the old system gave way to
feudalism. By the twelfth century, it was true of France
and England that lords held their land by conquest and
exempted themselves from taxation; the workers,
paying the taxes, were not permitted to carry arms.
Such an arrangement was always insecure because of the
desire of men to follow the old customs of land
inheritance. It was, Davis remarks, in the twelfth century, when England invaded Ireland, that English feudal
power was at its zenith. The Roman Catholic Church
reinforced that power; Pope Adrian granted Ireland to
Henry II in 1159. Davis is quick to note, however, that
toward the end of the sixteenth century, the English
Pale consisted of parts of five small counties. The rest of
Ireland, Celtic and Norman, followed gavelkind;
"primogeniture was regarded as a sin," he wrote. But
with Mountjoy's defeat of Hugh O'Neill in 1602, the
English conquest of Irish land was begun in earnest. It

was the breakdown of the Old Irish order and the beginning of England's troubles with Ireland. With persuasive power, Davis contrasts Ireland's woes to Norway's prosperity. In that country, despite changes in government, the social institutions were never destroyed and feudalism was never established. Social planners for Ireland should look to Norway for a correction of nineteenth-century Irish ills.

Any thought of inducing the absentee English land-lords to return to Ireland would be futile, Davis tells the Anglo-Irish readers of *The Citizen* in "Udalism and Feudalism." Since the English lord will not change his religion and the Irish worker will not change his, the presence of an alien lord will not remedy the situation. Davis would not "wish to change the faithful, pure, natural, affectionate Irishman into that animal, John Bull." Echoing Carlyle's sentiments about the dehumanizing effects of industrialization, Davis goes on to contradict the idea that Ireland must be assimilated to England. It would also be futile to attempt the other methods of curing the sick Irish economy: emigration and extermination. Davis's reply to the latter is short—"Try It!" To the former he asks, "Why emigrate?" Each year Ireland exports millions worth of food while the agrarian population is ill fed. Economically, it would not be profitable for the landlord to finance emigration, because the density of the population supports high rents, and England would not finance the transportation of Irishmen to Australia or Canada.

After discounting all the English notions for Anglicizing Irish agriculture, Davis argues for a system of proprietorship providing each farmer the right to own his land forever and pass it on to his children and his grandchildren. He insists that the ten- to twenty-year lease works against the land because the tenant will not enrich land only temporarily his own.

In *The Emigrants of Ahadarra* and *Valentine M'Clutchy*, William Carleton records in fiction what Thomas Davis records in "Udalism and Feudalism." Indeed, Carleton and Davis both indicate the need for a return to native industry. Davis, the more precise, offers two propositions:

> In proportion then to the permanence of his holding will be the caution with which the occupier will use the land, and the energy and care with which he will improve it.

> And further, ... in proportion to the interest which a stranger (be he tax gatherer, alien minister, or alien landlord) has in the crop and improvements, the motives for the tenant's industry will lessen.

Putting these two propositions together with rhetorical succinctness, Davis offers a solution to the land problem:

> Make a man's interest in his labour perfect and permanent, and you do the best to ensure his industry and wisdom as a labourer. That is, make him proprietor of the land he tills.

Davis, by writing "Udalism and Feudalism," identified Ireland's prime problem: land ownership. It is not surprising then that he joined Duffy and Dillon in establishing *The Nation* to correct social ills. From 1837, when *The Reform of the Lords* was published, Davis thought and wrote for political change and national sovereignty. Following his graduation he never

practiced law, because, he insisted, Ireland was a lawless
nation. Yet Davis used his legal training to plan for a
restructuring of Ireland, based on his knowledge of the
contemporary island.

The Patriot Parliament, a book-length work, rallies
the diverse Irish interests to create a vibrant nationalism
by recalling the optimistic time of Dublin, 1689. Re-
formers, Davis thinks, must look to the past for a way
to turn Irish defeats into victories. In this book he
parallels the events of the seventeenth century with
those of the nineteenth century. In 1843 enthusiasm for
the restoration of representative government and
sociopolitical liberties for Roman Catholics ran high. To
check it, charges of the unfitness of Irishmen to govern
themselves would be leveled. Davis discounted the
charges by demonstrating the patriotism of the Parliament of 1689. Although it favored King James over
William of Orange, the Irish Parliament denied the right
of an English one to legislate for Ireland. With much
pride, Davis also pointed out that religious equality was
established. Protestant prelates were supported by
Protestants; and Catholic prelates, by Catholics. No
Protestant prelates lost stipend or honor, and they
continued to sit in the Dublin Parliament. The legal
manner in which Davis details the composition of this
parliament and its laws is given emotional force by his
call for a spiritual rebirth of patriotism and peace.
Conquest, exile, confiscation, and slavery must give way
to cooperation, nativism, secure land tenure, and freedom. Clearly, Davis based his hope to end Ireland's
slavery and prepare for a permanent peace and prosperity on an important fact: Ireland was, is, and always
will be a separate kingdom, governed by its ancient

customs, laws, and traditions. As an Irish lawyer who
never practiced law, Davis was particularly struck by an
attempt of the patriot parliament of 1689 to abolish the
useless, idle, and expensive terms spent in London by
Irishmen before they were allowed to practice in their
native country.

In the Patriot Parliament, Davis gives us his ordered
sense of the reality of 1689; the work represents his
sense of the real optimism of pre-famine Ireland and of
the longings for freedom expressed by Daniel O'Connell
and his followers. But therein lies the great problem for
Davis. An Irish Catholic leader was evoking these
feelings, and the O'Connellites had to join forces with
the moderate Protestants before Ireland could be free.
Davis's argument embodied his vision of the Irish state
and of the men necessary for its rebirth, men cast in the
same mold as those of the patriot parliament.

It must be granted that Davis was not an original
thinker, he could not imagine a state different from his
idea of what ancient Ireland was before the first English
invasion by Henry II in the twelfth century. He sought
not to make a new state, but to remake Old Ireland,
conceived in terms of his personal sense of the past. His
originality was that he could make the analogy between
his own experiences in promoting nationalism and the
actions of the parliamentarians of 1689. As a student of
history, he could suggest that others join him in
establishing permanent peace for Ireland.

To English politicians determined to govern Ireland,
Davis was a traitor. To Irish politicians aspiring to
govern Ireland, he was a liberator. In declaring his
intent, Davis followed the course of earlier Irish
Protestants of 1689. He mined history to recover

Ireland's treasure, which was her moral superiority. This treasure, tarnished and tacky in 1843 when the *Patriot Parliament* was published, had to be restored to its natural brilliance. His work, Davis thought, would certainly add to the cause of a united Ireland where religion played an important role by *not* being a political issue.

After a five page preface, *The Patriot Parliament* has seven chapters: "A Retrospect," "Origin and Character of the Parliament — The House of. Lords," "The House of Commons," "The Session," "Repeal of the Act of Settlement," "The Act of Attainder," and "Conclusion." The opening sentence of the preface states Davis's purpose in preparing the story of the parliament of 1689 with its statutes, notes, and proceedings:

> This enquiry is designed to rescue eminent men and worthy acts from calumnies which were founded on the ignorance and falsehoods of the Old Whigs, who never felt secure until they had destroyed the character as well as the liberty of Ireland.

In the preface Davis then proceeds to link past slander of the parliamentarians with present slander of Daniel O'Connell's Catholic Emancipation Movement and the struggle for the Repeal of the Union. In fact, Davis remarks that any bold course of action that would free Ireland would evoke English backbiting, lies, and defamation of Irish character. In order to survive, English politicians in Ireland will always attempt to dishonor Irish statesmen, spurn Irish wisdom, and mock the valor of Irish soldiers in their fight for freedom. Davis is warning his fellow Irishmen of what they must face to achieve independence. If forewarned, he believes, they will be forearmed to capture the freedom that eluded the patriots of 1689 and Grattan's Parliament of 1782. After all, Davis writes, "The pedigree of our freedom is a century older than we thought." Look back, Davis says, to the parliament of 1689, which anticipated even more than that of 1782, for it enforced liberty of conscience, making it impossible to read the statutes of the parliament and know to which party, creed, or faction the majority belonged. This situation, of course, was what Davis dreamed of for Ireland in 1843. All creeds aside, let each Irishman prepare for a free Ireland with liberty of conscience paralleling political and civil liberties. In fact, his contemporaries should admire this parliament composed of Milesian (ancient Irish), Norman, Dane, and Anglo-Irish, and presided over by James II, for it was unique. No parliament of equal rank or national composition has sat in Dublin since; consequently, for the historian and the Irish patriot, this parliament demands respect and recognition.

There were books that favored the Parliament of 1689, Davis argues in his first chapter of *The Patriot Parliament:* Leslie's *Answer to King's State of Protestants* (1692), the primary source, followed by Curry's *Review of the Civil Wars of Ireland* (n.d.); Plowden's *Historical Review of Ireland* and *History of Ireland* (n.d.); and Jones's *Reply to an Anonymous Writer from Belfast, signed Portia* (1792). But there were books that slandered the Parliament: Archbishop King's *State of the Protestants* (1691) is the primary source, followed by Harris's *Life of King William* (1749) and Leland's *History of Ireland* (n.d.). King, in Davis's

opinion, is a stranger to the truth. His defamation of the
Irish peers was not supported by evidence, nor were his
complaints of the creation of the five new Lords.
Archbishop King also denounced the members of the
House of Commons because they were Catholics who
had wrested their positions from Protestants, but
Charles Leslie, also Protestant and son of the bishop of
Clogher, disputes King's claims.

Davis obviously goes to a great deal of trouble to
discredit the contemporary reporting of Archbishop
King. King received the bishopric of Derry from King
William before he published the *State of Protestants* and
after his short imprisonment in Dublin in 1689 by the
forces of King James II. Davis illustrates the bias of
Archbishop King, who so lacked objectivity that
another Protestant, Leslie, felt compelled to respond to
the lies in King's report, published "cum privilegio" by
King William's London printer. King's reporting, which
gave a distorted picture of Irish political life to English
readers, annoyed Davis because he recognized that
English public opinion of Irish politics was founded on
lies. The English, he was convinced, will always under-
estimate Irish wisdom and ability in governing Ireland if
fed a diet of slander about Irish political life. Since
Leslie's rebuttal went unanswered by King, who could
not offer any concrete evidence to support his lies,
Davis poses the question, "Why did anyone believe
King?" Davis answers when he states that Leslie's book
was suppressed along with other publications favoring
the Irish or King James II. Lies and slander were
necessary to establish an anti-Irish sentiment in London
and to discredit the allies of James in his bid to regain

his English throne. Anti-Irish feeling in London and English control of Ireland, Davis points out, caused the Anglo-Irish conflict and Irish political instability. There has always been an Archbishop King with the authority to disseminate propaganda while discrediting Irish opposition.

In the second chapter, Davis implies that if peaceful means could not effect Irish independence, then war would be justifiable to free Ireland. For instance, he remarks that laws were established for a permanent peace, but the parliamentarians prepared for a military crisis. Voting for large supplies for an army and navy, the members were ready to fight for an independent Ireland. Personally they recruited, armed, and trained troops for the eventual showdown with England. These legislator soldiers symbolize the noble nature of man, which abhors tyranny.

Looking into the future but learning from 1689, Davis recognized the need of military strength in securing independence; he was shrewder than O'Connell, who would not use violent means when parliamentary politics failed. (While O'Connell, as a Catholic lawyer, practiced his profession and argued for Irish rights, Davis, as a Protestant lawyer, refused to argue in the courts for rights that he knew had to be safeguarded by military action.) In developing his argument, Davis emphasizes the absolute superiority of force in maintaining civil and political liberty.

When James II landed at Kinsale, Ireland, on March 12, 1689, William and Mary had a month earlier been proclaimed King and Queen of England. Davis further notes in chapter two that James, escorted by D'Avaux, the French Ambassador, entered Dublin as a head of state. James issued proclamations that promised liberty of conscience for all subjects and called for a parliament in May. About three hundred men from the various Irish clans sat in Commons. Representatives from the old Catholic families of Plunket, Barnewell, Dillon, and Nugent sat beside the Protestant representatives of the Aungiers, Le Poers, and Forbes in the House of Lords. In unison, both houses attempted to restore justice to the native Catholic population, which suffered the same fate from fanatic Puritan Cromwellians between 1649 and 1660 as did Anglican Englishmen, namely, loss of life, land, and liberty. In 1641 Roman Catholics, despite the Elizabethan treachery and Ulster plantation of Protestants by James I after 1603, held two-thirds of Ireland. In 1680 they held but one-fifth. The remainder was owned by Protestant Englishmen who, after the Restoration of Charles II in 1660, gradually acquired land under his protection. Thus, between Protestant Cromwellians and Protestant Royalists, Ireland was divided in spirit, creed, and political views. Many Catholic Irishmen were now reduced to the tenantry or exiled.

In "The House of Commons," Davis states that Archbishop King's prejudiced "objection to the new constitution under King James's charters was the admission of Roman Catholics." The Dublin lawyer then notes that since there were 900,000 Catholic Irishmen and 300,000 Protestant Irishmen, it was natural to expect a greater number of Catholics in the Commons. He also calls attention to the sept representation:

Thus we see O'Neills in Antrim, Tyrone, Armagh; Magennises in Down; O'Reillys in Cavan; Martins, Blakes,

Kirwans, Dalys, Bourkes, for Connaught; MacCarthys, O'Briens, O'Donovans for Cork & Clare; Farrells for Lonford; Graces, Purcells, Butlers, Welshs, Fitzgeralds, for Tipperary, Kilkenny, Kildare, etc; O'Tooles, Byrnes, and Eustaces for Wicklow; MacMahons for Monaghan; Nugents, Bellews, Talbots, etc, for North Leinster.

As a lawyer knowledgeable in the ways of the parliamentary system, Davis details in the fourth chapter, on "The Session," the thirty-five acts that were passed by the parliament sitting for two months in Dublin. In an aside he writes, "We trust our readers will deal like searchers for truth. . . in a spirit enlightened by philosophy and warmed by charity." If his readers see that Irish factions could pull together in that awful hour, then why could not Irishmen in 1843 pull together for Irish political freedom? Davis tells the Williamite descendants, Jacobites, Catholics, and Protestants to look at the causes of past feuds and discover that much can be said for each faction. Furthermore, half of what each calls crime in the other is his own distrust of his neighbor's ignorance. "Knowledge, Charity, and Patriotism," Davis states, "are the only Powers which can loose this Prometheus – land. Let us seek them daily in our hearts and conversation." He then resumes the history of the session and its laws.

The parliamentarians of 1689 went about the business of establishing law. The acts, like Leslie's *Answer to King's State of the Protestants,* were suppressed by William's parliament. In fact, copies of the acts were ordered to be burned and became extremely scarce. Davis delights in telling us that he is reprinting those acts, which "ought to possess the very greatest interest for the historian and the patriot." One of these important acts states that the English Parliament can not bind Ireland; another removes unjust laws against the native Catholics; still another act provides for payment of tithes by Protestants to the Protestant Church and by Catholics to the Catholic Church — "a settlement of the church question," Davis injects, "fairer and more reasonable than the one adopted in our own day." Far-reaching and comprehensive in nature, other acts created fair trade practices with the colonies, regulated church practices, provided social welfare, and repealed odious acts that were not for the good of Ireland but for the good of England.

Davis begins the fifth chapter by stating that no act of the Irish Parliament of 1689 received such attention as the Repeal of the Act of Settlement. Both the Lords and Commons introduced bills to rectify the injustices wrought by Cromwell's unprincipled distribution of Irish property. In 1665, the Act of Settlement sanctioned the Puritan control in Ireland by legally transferring lands of the Irish natives to military colonists because the Restorationists obligated the Cromwellians to give up but one-third of the property they had earlier seized from the inhabitants. The effect of the Act of Settlement, Davis writes, "confirmed by law the Cromwellian robbery."

The repeal of such legislation, Davis argues, had wide-ranging consequences. Consideration had to be given to the people who leased, subdivided, and improved the properties, but had done so knowing that the property had been acquired by violence and treachery. The original owners and their families, awaiting the first opportunity to regain their property, had to be reckoned with. Another class to be considered was the Irish, who could go to "Hell or Connaught" and chose Connaught, with rights to their former lands. Finally there was the class of "adventurers" who received land during the Cromwellian regime and had its ownership legalized by the Act of Settlement. Davis, I think, shows his humanitarian attitude when he writes of this class that "however guilty the adventurers were when they came to Ireland, their families had been in it for thirty or forty years, and had time and some citizenship in their favour."

In general, Davis commends the way in which the parliament handled the claims of these groups. The Repeal Act restores to the Roman Catholics or their heirs the ancient properties and estates that "belonged to them or their Ancestors on 22 day of October, 1641." Those who fled to Connaught were to regain their estates, and the Cromwellian military colonization was to be voided. Current leases, however, were to be honored. The upheaval would have been felt by the landowners rather than by the working majority.

While Thomas Davis praises the patriots of 1689, he does not include all their acts in his praise. For example, he can not accept the Attainder Act. Writing always in the first-person plural to include his co-patriots, he tells his readers in "The Act of Attainder" that "we heartily censure this Attainder Act. It was the mistake of the Irish Parliament." This act would accuse Williamites of treason. Those attainted were in nine cases out of ten already in arms against James, but still it was an error in judgment, because it forced the Williamites and their children to bind themselves to the Dutch Protestant.

Since the traitors had already fled Ireland, the act could not be enforced until the Jacobites were victorious. At that time, it would be "needless and cruel to execute."

Furthermore, the ensuing Attainder Acts split Ireland into more factions, spreading the seeds of disunity that Davis believed to be a source of the current social unrest. Anti-Williamite Protestants and the Catholic majority were seeking solutions in 1843 to the problems that evolved from the atrophy of social justice while the eighteenth-century Penal Laws were in effect. In retrospect, then, the parliamentarians of 1689 were morally superior to the Williamites.

From this brief description it is evident that Davis had a prophetic insight and blamed Ireland's woe upon the failure of 1689. In 1843 Davis saw the analogy between the failure of the parliamentarians of 1689 to secure political independence and the failure of the Repealers to secure political independence. He also wondered why, in spite of the lessons of history, sociopolitical injustice prevailed. There was still no system to maintain sociopolitical justice, and it must be established if the strengths of old modes of moral thinking are to be preserved. Otherwise, the corrupt patterns and structure will continue to thwart a nation's search for justice and will destroy its moral and cultural values.

By way of concluding *The Patriot Parliament,* Davis admits "the many defects in our information and way of treating the subject. . . communicating our difficulties and offering our solutions, as they occurred to us, in hopes that some of our countrymen would take up the same study. . . and take the helm from us, and guide the

ship himself [*sic*] ." He was astute enough to reason that
the breakdown in communication between the many
factions in Irish life caused the loss of political freedom.
In presenting facts about King James's Irish Parliament
of 1689, Thomas Davis was preaching primarily for the
moral Protestant Ascendency.

To reach this class, Davis reviews the history of
sixteenth-century Ireland. The century, he says, "began
with civil, religious, and social persecutions, combining
all the atrocities to which Ireland had been alternately
subject for four centuries and a half." Then partial
insurrection, flamed by a rapacious government, was
followed by war, which saw royalists against royalists.
Service by patriots was undone by factious theologians,
followed by "conquest, slaughter, exile, confiscation
and slavery." Then an English Restoration, which gave
the crown its worst prerogatives without returning the
royalists their property, was followed by a settlement in
which English fanatics, blasting Irish character, drove
their King to Ireland. In 1689 civil war was raging in
Ireland, and the Dutchman on the English throne would
be preparing an invasion of Ireland if it harbored the
deposed monarch. Davis reminds his readers that these
Irishmen were in an untenable position. They had to
assert their independence and right to self-government
without any English claim upon them while simultane-
ously establishing King James II upon the English
throne. These men had to protect a refugee King while
protecting their distinct nationality from the avarice and
greed of some of the English aristocracy. By painting
such a black picture, Davis makes the troubles of 1843
appear minor compared to the problems facing the

people of 1689. Surely the patriots of 1843 could match the deeds of the patriots of 1689 in their establishment of order. Of greater value, though, was their establishment of a code for the "permanent liberty and prosperity of Ireland."

Davis, at once lawyer and politician, in summing up his argument for a free Ireland pleads his case before Protestant Irishmen. He asks, "Is not this [Parliament of 1689] an epitome of the Protestant patriot attempts. . . . Is not this the soul of '82?" He answers in the affirmative. The spirit of 1689 is the spirit of 1782 and the hope of 1843. Davis's rhetoric calls for a united Ireland, and the bid for union must emanate from his co-religionists. Davis refuses to accept the indignities of Irish law and particularly praises the lords and commons of '89 for creating Irish Inns of Court and attempting to establish the supremacy of Irish law. He makes it clear that keeping terms in London as a prerequisite for practicing Irish Law is distasteful, expensive, and demoralizing. Think, Davis says, of the absurdity of hauling off future Irish advocates and judges "to a foreign and dissolute capital to go through an idle and expensive ceremony, term after term, as an essential to being allowed to practice in the courts of this their native kindgom."

Noting in his conclusion that the torch of national independence passed from Molyneux, to Swift, to Lucas, to Hood, to Grattan, Davis says something escaped the eighteenth-century politicians: the navy needed to protect the coast and the army needed to scathe the invaders. Consequently, the coast of nineteenth-century Ireland "had no guardian and our

desecrated fields knew no avenger." He asks then that
some persons will be found in the future who will
restore the vigor of the Parliament and establish armed
forces to insure national independence.

Unfortunately, Davis lacked O'Connell's oratorical
skill and his audience was limited to the readers of the
scholarly *Patriot Parliament.* The much greater medium,
public address, was within O'Connell's realm. Davis,
directing his message to the minority who could read,
evoked a slower response and was seriously handicapped
in his role as liberator. The Irish people could always
precisely express their sociopolitical ills. In addition,
they knew when they were oppressed, but they could
not cure themselves. As diagnosticians, the Irish people
were infallible; as therapeuticians, they were ineffective.
Moreover, accustomed to ancient laws and customs of
social justice administered by a responsible aristocracy,
the Irish people now lacked such an aristocracy.
Through newspapers and books Davis tried to supply
leadership and information to enable people to make
wise decisions while O'Connell used his oratorical skill
to define and attempt resolution of Ireland's problem.
There were thus two distinct informational systems at
work prior to the Revolution of 1848, but no means of
coordinating them. The end result was that only a
partial solution to the problem was reached. As Davis
was developing a historian's view of England's misrule of
the Irish state, O'Connell was past his prime in offering
assistance to the young Irelander. There was really no
opportunity for Davis and O'Connell to integrate their
distinct skills and overthrow the old coercive political
structures. The educated Protestant might read and be

moved by Davis's moral vision in the *Patriot Parliament,* and the working Irish Catholic might listen and be moved by O'Connell's eloquence, but where was the professional who could coordinate their efforts? That individual did not exist.

Consequently, the Irish people on the verge of a revolution in 1843 were hardly prepared to confront a secretive governmental structure that functioned effectively. It was the professional in Dublin Castle who could see the divisive nature of the rebellion and play one nationalist against the other to thwart their united action. The Dublin government, whose mission it was to retain the governing powers, worked amorally to retain its position. In order to change that position, both Davis and O'Connell had to overcome a superior informational system employed by Dublin officials. Historical data and contemporary rhetoric, however, were ineffective against a government that could pay for pertinent political information or fabricate it when needed. It could be concluded, then, that Davis's *The Patriot Parliament* was not worth his effort. That opinion, I think, would be incorrect, because his analysis of the political events of 1689 guided later nationalists.

Davis's editing of John Philpot Curran's speeches reveals an interest in Curran's participation in the Irish political system. Obviously, Davis admired Curran and applauded his sense of nationality. However, the songs and essays written for *The Nation* do more than applaud another Irishman's sentiments; they dramatize Davis's drive for national distinction.

2
Prose for The Nation

Davis wrote essays for *The Nation* on a wide variety of topics, but his essays on Irish song, education, painting, and the peasantry demonstrate his unique contribution to the nationalist paper. In particular, his writing on songs and ballads reveals that he was appealing to the average Irishman to recognize the value of traditional Irish airs and lyrics and to compose contemporary music in their fashion. Davis believed that songs have their place in nation-making, and he wrote two essays on the subject for *The Nation,* on December 21, 1844, and January 4,1845.

In the first essay on "Irish Songs," he has much to say about the Irish gift of song, believing it to be greater than that of the English, Italian, or Spanish, but below that of the Scots. Davis was pleasantly surprised to find how many good songs were available for his projected edition of Irish songs. He rejects the current "cabbage and artificial flowers called Harps and Shamrocks and Minstrels" for the more dignified works of Banim, Lover, Griffin, Callanan, Father Prout, Mangan, Furlong, Maginn, Lady Morgan, Curran, Drennan, Orr. English songs, he thinks, are the "worst in the world." England has no one to sing of her greatest glory—the

Royal Navy; those songs she has are for the opera, not
the forecastle. Ironically, the one good English naval
song "The Arethusa," he says (mistakenly), was written
by Mr. Hoare, an Irishman. The words are set to
Carolan's air—"The Princess Royal." "English robbery
of Irish literature is quite as marked as of Irish wealth,"
Davis writes. There is really no spirit in English love
songs either, according to Davis. If such songs were
written for Irish or Scot girls, they would despise their
lovers.

Davis likes the songs of the Scots because they are
"full of heart and reality," emanating from an "intense
passion, simple taste, and heroic state of society." He
wants Irish songs to be of that nature and criticizes
some of Thomas Moore's songs because they are
"pretty, too refined, subtle in dialect, and too negligent
of narrative." When Moore's songs lack vehemence or
omit the sterner passions, he does not regard them as
good, but he does admit that Moore is Ireland's greatest
poet. Yet Davis objects to Moore's selection of material,
feeling he did not write for the poor and middle-class
Irishman. An Irish poet must write for every class. Such
poets must be of "bounding animal spirits," passion-
ately loved, and "ere philosophy raised them above it,
ardently hated." They must also be "generous in
friendship, maddened by strong sounds, sobbing with
unused strength and fiery for freedom and glory." Davis
is actually cataloguing his own qualifications and
describing the nationalist passion that ruled him. He is
asking Irish poets of every religious creed and racial
stock to sing noble thoughts for a united Ireland.

In the second part of the essay on "Irish Songs,"

Davis rejects the irregular, structured songs of the eighteenth century with their slavish and despairing grief, reckless joy, religious bitterness, and tireless allegory. He expects his contemporaries to forge a new link, which would place Irish song clearly in Carolan's earlier tradition of pure melody and meaning. Irish song writers from the eighteenth century who preserved local historical events and sang of human love, joy, war, and mourning could in the meantime supply the need for song, though their work would have to be abridged, inasmuch as their thoughts were for libraries, not cabins.

When Davis suggests an editing and reissue of past Irish songs, he is being pragmatic because so few of the working majority lived in an environment that would allow them to appreciate the aesthetic quality of the old masters. But even if they could not appreciate the subtle, sophisticated verse, they could still appreciate the historic or narrative line of a truncated version of the past poets of Ireland. Davis notices one aspect of the Old Irish songs that bothers him, namely, that there are no truly national songs. While they are national in form and theme, they are clannish in opinion. The songs celebrate the deeds of the O'Neills, O'Mores, O'Connors, or McCarthys, but they do not sing of an Irish nation. On the contrary, the songs may preclude any national sentiment and decry the Irishness or "more than Irish" feelings of neighbors in the same way that they denounce foreign oppressors. Davis admits that he was startled to learn that in the seventeenth century, when Ireland was surely subject to Norman and Saxon rule, the bards cried to the once-invading Milesians of pre-Christian Ireland for help. They did not try to

Hibernicize the current aristocracy. Nationality was genealogical rather than geographic. If you were not of the ancient Irish race and your family had been in Ireland for only a few generations, you still were not Irish. Nonsense, writes Davis, for the Milesians were not progenitors of the seventeenth-century clans. But since old invaders belonged to a class of conquerors that constituted the aristocracy of ancient Ireland, they were fit subjects for heroic national poetry. Davis refers to them in his "Lament for the Milesians" as proud "chieftains of green Inis-Fail," and all Irish creeds and classes are "heirs of their rivers, their sea and their land." To suggest that the Milesians are ancestor to a particular clan or chieftain subverts the concept of nationality that Davis had in mind. In this instance, he demonstrates one cause of Irish disunity. Clan loyalty rather than nationality was one phase of the traditional Irish way of life that the eighteenth-century poets nourished. The older idea of the "ardrigh" or high King who kept the clans from warfare was too remote for their poetic songs. The Penal Laws, effective and terrible, allowed the poets to imagine a chieftain appearing from the demoralized remnants of a proud and noble clan, but a high King was beyond their poetic vision.

In his "Irish Songs" Davis argues that Irish Ireland and Anglo-Irish Ireland must coalesce. Nineteenth-century poets must restore the notion of nationality. Noting that Dr. Mac Hale had translated Moore into Irish, Davis indicates that the people did not like the result, possibly because Moore's poems lacked the idiom of the people's speech and thoughts. Davis longs for the day when someone born and reared in the Irish environment will sing for all who have settled on Irish ground. In the interval, he will be satisfied if the best of Moore, Griffin, Banim, Callanan, and Drennan are printed. They should be available to the English-speaking Irishmen to counteract the coarse, slanderous, cheap ballads that are available. Printers in Dublin, Drogheda, Cork, and Belfast live by their sale of vulgar ballads, which should be discontinued. Davis wants good ballads on good paper for the masses.

Davis would also dismiss the Anglo-Irish songs of the eighteenth century because they are "indecent or factious." The Protestant cadets, living in southern Ireland as garrision soldiers, wrote the indecent songs. They were crammed with reference to drinking, racing, and dancing — the social life of an occupying army. "The Rakes of Mallow" is one such indecent song. The Ulster Presbyterian clergy wrote the factious songs. While their songs are "vigorous and musical," the subject matter is not fit for the young Ireland generation inasmuch as it counters all notion of a union between Catholics and Protestants. It will be impossible for a comprehensive nationality to emerge from the various sectors of Irish life if Ulster songs like "The Protestant Boys" remain in vogue.

As Davis saw it, Protestant Irishmen during Grattan's era, when the Volunteers of 1782 supplied the muscle for nationalism, had great opportunity to write excellent songs. The times were ripe for national songs to be picked from any tree, but pickers never materialized. The one good Volunteer song, Davis says, was written by Lysaght. Davis does not identify the song, but it is probably "The Man, Who Led the Van of Irish Volunteers," sung to the melody of "The British Grenadiers."

To compose an Irish song, Davis tells his readers in "Irish Songs," one must become familiar with the variety of Irish airs and listen to them over and over again before writing words to them. Davis does warn the public of two dangers, though. First, since the Irish airs in Moore's melodies are corrupt, they should not be used for study. Lover's tunes are even more corrupt, and they should also be avoided. Second, since there are hundreds of fine Irish airs to which no English words have been written, contemporary songwriters should not write words to those melodies to which Moore or Griffin have already written "moderately good words." The would-be Irish songwriter should go on from there.

In trying to study the old Irish airs, Davis tells his readers that they should get at the character of the music, which depends upon the tempo. The music may express many moods: "gay, hopeful, loving, sentimental, lively, hesitating, woeful, despairing, resolute, fiery or variable." "In all cases," Davis writes, "the tune must suggest, and will suggest, to the lyricist the sentiment of the words." He then gives more practical advice. For instance, he says that the tune will fix the number of lines in a verse, but oftentimes the number and order of the lines may vary. One long line can be written instead of two short lines where the first line has accents on both the last syllables. It is also very important to have rhyming words where the same notes are emphasized at the ends of musical phrases. He rather likes the use of double rhymes for political and didactic songs, because political English words, usually derived from Latin, are long, with double accents. Expletive syllables at the beginning of the line, adding to the effect of a gay tune, must not follow a double rhyme. If at all possible, in rousing songs one syllable for every note should be used. But one syllable-one note would not be too pleasant to the English ear because of the harshness created by a grouping of consonants. This is what Mary Kelly Carleton meant when she told her son William that the English words were not suitable for Irish airs. She did not know why they were not suitable; she knew only that a discordant effect resulted from the wedding of English words to Irish music. Davis, in analyzing the situation, was able to pinpoint the difficulty and explain why hundreds of Irish tunes lacked English verses. Despite the difficulty, young writers should attempt the task. In closing "Irish Songs," he offers a hypothesis:

> If men able to write, will fling themselves gallantly and faithfully on the work we have here plotted for them, we shall soon have Fair and Theatre, Concert and Drawing-Room, Road and Shop, echoing with songs bringing home Love, Courage, and Patriotism to every heart.

Davis wrote to cool the passionate heat that his concept of nationality radiated and to arouse his countrymen. The nature of nationality was something that had occupied Davis ever since his years in Trinity College. I think that Davis was trying to define *nation,* the life of a nation, and the force of nationalism in the lives of all Irishmen. He never doubted his national faith, but he sought answers to the perplexing questions that other Anglo-Irishmen asked. If *nation* signified a united common bond of ideas, hopes, and expectations, then could he see Ireland as a nation? If the life of a nation meant the vital articulation of laws, and a sustained assertion of Christianity's divine mission, then dare Davis see Ireland come to life? If the lives of all Irishmen were subject to this notion of nation, then would Ireland be a "nation once again?"

In the reality of his century, *a nation* did signify that a common tie bound the citizens to a mutually satisfactory system that reiterated abstract principles in a concrete way. In other words, ideas, hopes, and expectations had to be brought together imaginatively so that the practical affairs of everyday life could be carried out with the security of internal authority. Nationality existed in England where geography made all citizens Englishmen, but such was not the case in Ireland. Ideas from O'Connell and his class of Catholics clashed with ideas from Davis and his class of Protestants. Ulster Presbyterians hoped for a place in the Irish sun that would displace both Munster Protestants and Irish Catholics. The Protestant Ascendency expected to retain its superior economic position while Catholic insurgents were battling to get a foot on the ladder to economic success. Internal authority that could control these forces did not exist. Such an authority had to be vested in a person, a place, and a principle. During Davis's public life, the idea of nation was a complex creative process. No single individual understood and could control the process. O'Connell and later William Smith O'Brien — the former Catholic, the latter Protestant — were recognized as national leaders, but they lacked place and coherent principles. The Dublin Castle would have to be seized and principles set down — as Luther nailed his 95 theses on the castle church door at Wittenberg, as the Americans composed their Declaration of Independence at Independence Hall — and as, one must add, the Irish poets and patriots would disseminate the Proclamation and storm the General Post Office in 1916.

Thomas Davis tried to effect a coalition, but he did not live long enough to issue a summons and proclaim a constitutional government. More astute than O'Connell, he gave up the idea of reforming the House of Lords and realized that he had to develop a sense of nationality by disclosing to Irish and Anglo-Irish the beauty of Irish culture. "Irish Song" was one essay to that point. Davis envisioned the birth of a nation as an evolutionary process, the first stage of which was the bonding of different cultural elements. The final stage would have to be the establishment of political power that would hold the elements in place. Both stages would demand a change in the educational system, and Davis addressed himself to this difficult task on more than one occasion.

Education was to nationality as match was to fire, according to Davis. To illustrate the connection, he wrote five essays in *The Nation:* "Self-Education," February 18, 1843; "Popular Education," July 27, 1844; "Educate that You May Be Free," October 5, 1844; "Study," February 8, 1845; and "Academical Education," May 17, 1845. These essays insist that social happiness depends upon a sound system of education.

When Davis wrote "Self-Education" in 1843, he was

extending the argument on "The Utility of Debating Societies in Remedying the Defects of University Education" that he presented to the Trinity College Historical Society in 1839. Davis, a university graduate, knew that a university education could be a severe handicap to an Irishmen because of the bias bred in the bone of the curriculum. He opens the essay with a long quote from Goethe, of which one sentence illustrates Davis's aesthetic concept:

> Men are so inclined to content themselves with what is commonest; the spirit and the senses so easily grow dead to the impressions of the beautiful and the perfect; that everyone should study to nourish in his mind the faculty of feeling these things by every method in his power.

The search for beauty, then, is a worthwhile quest and every individual has the power to make the journey. In "Self-Education" Davis tells his readers how and where to educate themselves. "Home," he writes, "is the great teacher; and its teaching passes down in honest homes from generation to generation." In these homes decorum, cleanliness, order, respect for the aged, affection without passion, truth, piety, and justice are learned. Because the National Schools are so poor, Davis says the "people must take diligent care to procure books on the history, men, language, music, and manners of Ireland for their children." He closes the essay by stating that thinking cannot be deputized; the Irish "people must think for themselves."

Davis prepared "Popular Education" for *The Nation* to recognize three great Irish schoolmasters: the National Board, the Press, and the Repeal Association, each with its own responsibility. The spirit and the sagacity that motivated men in these institutions should inspire the populace. Maps, books, prints, and brochures on Irishmen, deeds, scenes, resources, and arts of Ireland would provide neighborhoods with native information. Such knowledge would generate patriotism. An illiterate population, hopelessly enslaved, cannot be nation-minded. "In this unfortunate country, where over three million seven hundred thousand persons over five years old can neither read nor write," Davis points out, "1,400,000 can only read but not write, and less than half a million can both read and write." With the total population of Ireland about eight million, the urgency of Davis's concern for educational reform is understandable. Since he was a writer and not an eloquent speaker, it can also be understood why Davis's effect on the national movement was greater toward the end of the nineteenth century than during his lifetime. He knew that a literate population could produce a political system, but it took time to accomplish the process.

Davis links education with political freedom in his essay "Educate, That You May Be Free." By drawing an analogy between Ireland and Prussia, he shows how education makes the difference between a province and a nation. Prussia's offices, colleges, schools, and troops could be destroyed, but within six months the civil and military institutions could be restored because of stored knowledge. New offices, schools, and armies could be organized once a central authority was recognized by the Prussians. Davis says that even with a central authority, Ireland could not set up an ordered sociopolitical structure because civil, military, and general knowledge is lacking among all classes. "It was to the interest of our ruler to keep us ignorant, that we might be weak." England, Davis cries out, kept Ireland ignorant by first prohibiting education; then refusing to provide for it; next, by perverting it into an organ of bigotry; and finally, by stunting it in an anti-national way. Davis makes it clear in the next breath that by arguing for education he is not arguing against immediate independence. No. Political independence would be the best teacher, and it is the duty of the educated minority to change the state of ignorance that makes Ireland a weak province. While it is true Davis writes, that millions have much to learn, thousands have much to teach. They may do so via the Repeal Reading Rooms. The Repeal Association will supply the newspapers, books, and maps for these rooms if they are truly educational centers and not gossip shops. With embarrassment Davis reports that ten Irish counties are without a single bookseller; he asks the readers of *The Nation* to remedy that disgrace. Besides working through the Repeal Association, educated Irishmen, in their effort to broaden the educational base and secure political freedom, can join societies that promote agriculture, manufacturing, art, and literature. Books are so cheap now, Davis says, that poverty is no excuse for ignorance.

Wise enough to know that the possession of books does not make the man, Davis wrote "Study" for *The Nation* on February 8th, 1845, to offer study habits to young men searching for knowledge. Referring to Carlyle, Davis says that Carlyle thinks a library is the true University of their day. The Anglo-Irishman, agreeing with the Anglo-Scotsman, thinks that a creative spirit must accompany the quest for book learning. Otherwise, the student would become a bookworm, losing his simplicity without gaining strength. He could also become weary from reading shallow, idle, impertinent, and extravagant books. Davis warns the ardent student of danger: the yearning for universal knowledge. If he tries to learn everything, he will skim many things. As a reading clinician, Davis spots and treats another malady: the consumption of two volumes of novels or biographies a day when the reader might better be working or playing. If a reader wishes to acquire knowledge for future use, he should be selective. Epic reading, Davis says, is the highest form of reading; he defines it, without pausing to examine the artistic excellence of a narrative work, as the curious concern for a hero's fate. Scientific reading, on the other hand, is pragmatic. A skilled reader must be both an epic and a scientific reader. Believing that analytical or critical reading can lead to a "miserable state of soul," Davis remarks that a living man or a man of strong character will rarely adopt that pose because the creative power to combine new ideas or notice unknown combinations is greater than the ability to distinguish and separate.

To develop that strong character, Davis wrote "Academical Education" for *The Nation* on May 17, 1845, less than four months before his death. He rejects separate but equal education for Catholics and Protestants, advocating mixed education because it is "consistent with piety, and favorable to that union of Irishmen of different sects, for want of which Ireland is in rags and chains." Davis argues for an educational system that would unite the country. Because he was a product of the exclusive Anglo-Irish Protestant system, he knew the bias, bigotry, and defects of its exclusive education. An exclusive Catholic educational system would, in Davis's opinion, develop its own bias and bigotry. Mixed educational institutions would be superior to either exclusively Protestant or Catholic Schools; they would acquaint all with Ireland's ancient artistic heritage and prepare students to live together peacefully.

In less than two years Davis worte seven essays on Irish painting: "Hints for Irish Historical Paintings," July 29, 1843; "National Art," December 9, 1843; "A Gallery of Casts," December 23, 1844; "The Irish Art Union," December 14, 1844; and "Irish Pictures," April 19, 1845. His national bias, evident in each essay, set parameters for Irish artists. Ireland's magnificent scenery and long history should be the material for artists, who should paint the topography and historical figures of Ireland. In "Irish Pictures," for instance, Davis catalogues the fit subjects for artists:

> The Druid in his grove – the Monk in his abbey – the Creaght on his hill – the Pagan Conqueror – the Christian liberator – the Norman castle with its courted maidens, its iron barons, and its plumed train – the Irish rath with its circling trench, and circling woodland, its patriarch prince, its Tartar clan, its foster-love and its harping bards – the Dane in his galley – the Viceroy in his council – the Patriot in his forethought – the Martyr in his endurance – the Hero in his triumph—

Artists, according to Davis, have an important role in creating a national consciousness and Irish ones should give up painting and working in England because there is a need for native historical paintings.

Paradoxically, Davis writes in "Hints for Irish Historical Paintings" that there are "Irish artists, but no Irish, no national art . . . it is injurious to the artists, and disgraceful to the country." To remedy that situation, he prints a list of historical events that were suggested by a friend as material for Irish painting. Davis then offers to print "any suggestions on the subject." His list begins with the landing of the Milesians, goes through Nial and his nine hostages, St. Patrick before the Druids at Tara, Brian Boru reconnoitering the Danes before Clontarf, Shane O'Neill at Elizabeth's Court, O'Sullivan crossing the Shannon, James's entry into Dublin, Liberty Boys reading a Drapier's letter, Curran cross-examining Armstrong, O'Connell speaking in a Munster Chapel, Conciliation—Orange and Green, and ends with the lifting of the Irish flags of a National Fleet and Army. Davis wants the action to be obvious and the dress, arms, architecture, and characters to be historically accurate. Current social life, Davis adds, could be illustrated if the artist read the Poor Report or the stories from Carleton, the Banims, and Griffin. The best source, though, for contemporary action, he suggests, would be personal observation.

In other essays, Davis pleads for artistic merit and integrity but for the greater glory of Ireland. Interestingly, he believes that state patronage is more beneficial than private patronage because private patrons do not encourage great works. From Athens, to Rome, to the Low Countries, Davis says that the state produced great artists and there is no reason why an Irish government should not follow that example.

Davis's concern with Irish artists and heroic subjects
did not mean, however, that he was blind to the sordid
life of the rural Irish in their daily battle with usurers,
corrupt land agents, absentee landlords, and a rigged
system of land tenure. His thoughts on these subjects
were expressed in "The State of the Peasantry" (May
24, 1845). "In a climate soft as a mother's smile, on a
soil fruitful as God's love," Davis writes, "the Irish
peasant mourns." His humanism, clearly expressed in
this essay, describes the misery of the poor farmers in
chimneyless cabins with rotten roofs, clay walls, and
dirt floors. If the infants survive, they must face a life of
hard labor for poor wages, hoping to acquire another
cabin, furnished with a cooking pot, a table, a few chairs
and stools, straw bedding and then to inherit their
parents' enemies — "the landlord, tax gatherer, and the
law." The essay is addressed to the ruling class:

> Aristrocracy of Ireland, will ye do nothing? — Will ye do
> nothing for fear — for pity — for love? Will ye forever
> abdicate the duty and the joy of making the poor
> comfortable . . . . We warn and entreat you to consider the
> State of the Peasantry, and to save them with your own
> hands.

Other essays also reveal Davis's deep and com-
prehensive concern for things Irish: "Absenteeism of
Irish Genius," "Sea Kings," "Hy-Fiachrach," "Skulls of
the Irish," "Irish History," "O'Donovan's Irish Gram-
mar," "Our National Language," "Monuments of
Ireland," "Irish Topography," "Industrial Resources of
Ireland," "Irish Antiquities and Irish Savages,"
"Ireland's People," "The Valuation of Ireland," "Irish

Scenery," "Old Ireland," "Foreign Travel," "Speeches of Grattan," "The Round Towers of Ireland," "Institutions of Dublin," "The Library of Ireland," "Wexford," "Commercial History of Ireland," and "The Irish Brigade." Clearly, Davis used *The Nation* as an educational device to bring before its readers an accurate accounting of Ireland past, present, and future. Ranging over a large field, he ploughed well and planted national seeds that germinated in the fertile souls of starved men, women, and children. Nourished by other generations, the harvest was slow to mature and ripen. But when it did, it was "Davis All Ireland."

3
Poetic Contributions to The Nation

In the fall of 1841, at a meeting of the Repeal Association that convened to urge the repeal of the 1801 Union with Britain, Thomas Davis met Charles Gavan Duffy, a Belfast journalist and editor of the *Vindicator,* a biweekly newspaper. In the spring of 1842 the two met again, this time joined by John Blake Dillon, another Catholic journalist. Discovering that they had a common cause, these three men thought of establishing a weekly paper, neither Whig nor Tory but nationalistic. The final arrangements for *The Nation* were made, and the first number was out on October 15, 1842, one day after Davis's twenty-eighth birthday. The novelty of combining literature with news, opinions, and Irish matters added to the instant success of the paper.

For the sixth number, Davis supplied a ballad, the "Lament of Eoghan Ruadh O'Neill," which initiated his poetic career. The poetry pleased his readers and himself, releasing his ego from the restraints of a

consciously structured essay or rhetorical address. Take
the introduction to O'Neill's lament:

> Did they dare, did they dare, to slay
> Eoghan Ruadh O'Neill?
> Yes, they slew with poison him they feared
> to meet with steel.

That is a commanding beginning. In his prose writings
Davis often posed and answered questions, but in poetic
composition, the question and answer device—evoking a
ballad convention that can be powerfully dramatic—
took on an added ironic dimension. Here his opening
question must have shocked his readers, have involved
them in a dramatic and intense experience.

As Davis's poetic career continued, other historical
events offered themes, and the pedantry of *The Reform
of the Lords* was replaced by the liveliness of his verse.
Indeed, the political unrest of the times evoked about
eighty poems in three years. His method of composition, according to Duffy, was inspirational. Davis wrote
as the thoughts came to him. At times he did not revise
his verse if the urgency of publication demanded a poem
or ballad for *The Nation.*

The majority of Davis's poetry is nationalistic; the
rest is love or nature poetry. The love poems express a
personal attitude not evident in the other poems or
prose. They include "A Christmas Scene or Love in the
Country," "Oh! The Marriage," "Maire Bhan a Stoir,"
"Eibhlin a Ruin," "Duty and Love," "Love's Longings,"
"The Bride of Mallow," "Annie, Dear," "The Boatman
of Kinsale," "A Plea for Love," "Love Chant," "Darling
Nell," and "Love and War."

To the music of "The Swaggering Jig," Davis wrote "Oh! The Marriage." In the first stanza the singer is identified as a young girl who has a faithful, loving suitor, Eoghan. He is described in the next stanza:

> His hair is a shower of soft gold,
> His eye is as clear as the day,
> His conscience and vote were unsold
> When others were carried away;
> His word is as good as an oath,
> And freely 'twas given to me;
> Oh! Sure 'twill be happy for both
> The day of our marriage to see.
> Then, oh! the marriage, etc.

Linking faithfulness in love to loyalty in politics, Davis celebrates Eoghan's clear conscience. His refusal to vote for the Union of 1801, distinguishes him from those who sold their vote — and, to Davis, their souls. Eoghan's morality is matched by the golden image of his clear-eyed beauty. He and his beloved are figures from an Edenic idyll: they will get by on his paltry possessions, and their life will be happy.

Another love poem, "Love's Longings," suggests an autobiographical parallel. As a suitor for Annie Hutton, Davis was not exactly the proper choice because of his unsettled income. A nationalist journalist, facing the responsibilities of marriage, had serious shortcomings: he could offer only love. The second stanza of "Love's Longings" — redeemed from banality by the ironic emphasis placed on death in the last line — describes Davis's relationship to Annie Hutton:

> I know I am not worthy

> Of one so young and bright,
> And yet I would do for thee
> Far more than others might.
> I cannot give you pomp or gold,
> If you should be my wife,
> But I can give you love untold,
> And true in death or life.

While "Love's Longings" is ostensibly not a great love poem, it evoked an emotional response from the readers of *The Nation.* Many of them contemplating marriage could offer no more than the speaker: a faithful and enduring love unmatched by financial security.

"Duty and Love," another love poem, has two stanzas of eight lines each. The first two lines ("Oh! lady, think not that my heart has grown cold,/If I woo not as once I could woo;") have a dramatic quality, arresting the reader's eye or the listener's ear. Sung to "My Lodging is on the Cold Ground," "Duty and Love" is provocative. The last stanza notes the lover's decision:

> But it is that my country's in bondage and I
>   Have sworn to shatter her chains!
> By my duty and oath I must do it or lie
>   A corpse on her desolate plains.
> Then sure dearest maiden 'twere sinful to sue,
>   And crueller far to win,
> But, should victory smile on my banner, to you
>   I shall fly without sorrow or sin.

All the women of Ireland who had waited in vain for the shattering of the nation's chains could share the lady's position. All the Irishmen who fought and delayed or postponed marriage could share the lover's predicament. Touching the commonest of cultural experiences, the poem compelled identification with the lady and the lover.

Not all patriotic Irishmen, however, were destined to postpone consummation of their love. Some married and maintained their independent attitudes, as characterized in "The Boatman of Kinsale."

> The brawling squires may heed him not,
>   The dainty stranger sneer—
> But who will dare to hurt our cot
>   When Myles.O'Hea is here?
> The scarlet soldiers pass along;
>   They'd like, but fear to rail;
> His blood is hot, his blow is strong—
>   The Boatman of Kinsale.

His wife willingly shares this life because she believes that "money never made the man, nor wealth a happy home." So, as long as he is loved and feels free, he will trust in God and remain a loyal husband. Bourgeois values idealized, to be sure, but all the more appealing to the popular mind for their simplicity!

Throughout Davis's love poems, we are aware of a dualistic conflict in the Irish social structure, as he sees it. On the one side are patriotic, moral, physically attractive, poor young lovers. On the other side are tyrannic, amoral, poorly sketched rich aristocrats. The members of the first class are the hope of Ireland, while the members of the second class are her destruction. Brave young men and women, often in gay moods, are poised for conflict with the aristocracy. But Davis does not characterize the lords and ladies who go about by carriage. The members of the Protestant Ascendency are faceless in Davis's love poetry; but the members of the politically faceless majority are named and remembered. The scenic wonders of their land are also minutely described. Harmony between people and place, consequently, exists. A certainty, rather than a wonder, about the balance between man and nature exists. Then, too, God in omnipotent splendor is part of the world of these poems.

Are Marie, Eileen, Annie, Nell, Eoghan, and the boatman real people or realistic depictions of possible characters? Do they represent the country people? Yes, and no. Yes, because they are without money and position; no, because they are romantically depicted, "noble savages" all. For a more accurate picture of the laboring agricultural class, one must read the fiction of William Carleton, Gerald Griffin, and John Banim. Therein one finds a sordid world of suffering people who have neither the organizational ability for a successful rebellion nor the money to finance one. Lovers do exist in the novels of these writers, but they differ from the Davis protrait. In Griffin's *Collegians,* the moral, pure, sweet young girl is murdered by her unfaithful lover; in Carleton's *Black Prophet,* the young lovers undergo a variety of hardships and only one couple acquires a small measure of prosperity. Banim's *Tales of the O'Hara Family* describes the strange, secret Irish world of Crohoore, who hacks to death his employers and escapes with their daughter. Davis substitutes for that horror an imaginary pastoral scene. Ireland's beauty, not her "terrible beauty" inspires him. Because Davis was not part of the suffering rural population that was experiencing starvation, social chaos, and political extermination, he idealized the country people. He felt their desire to lead a better life and encouraged them to do so. Survival on a potato diet was their lot; a romantic interlude along a river bank with a husband having hair "a shower of soft gold" was a sheer fantasy of their existence and Davis's love poetry is nearly always more fantasy than reality. No doubt it offered pleasure and a relief from the pain in the fiction of Carleton, Griffin, and Banim.

The poetry describing the natural beauty of Ireland is associated with particular people and places. It is important to realize that God, man, and nature are at peace with one another in Davis's poems. The arbitrary English categorization of nineteenth-century poetry into Romantic or Victorian can not be made to apply to a Davis poem. He was composing for Ireland that very body of verse which Wordsworth, Coleridge, Byron, Shelley, Keats, Browning, Tennyson, and Hardy composed for England. Davis, like Emerson, Thoreau, Lowell, Irving, Cooper, Longfellow, Poe, and Simms, breathed his soul into a national literature.

In his "Preface to the Second Edition of the Lyrical Ballads" (1800), Wordsworth says that a poet is duty bound "to choose incidents and situations from common life." Furthermore, each poem must have a "worthy purpose," and the poet write under one restriction only, namely, the necessity of giving immediate pleasure, which arises from the poet's possession of information that is passed on, man to man and differently from the way in which a doctor, lawyer, astronomer, or natural philosopher would transfer facts. In his poetry, Davis moves away from the lawyer's realm to that of the poet, evoking pleasure, man to man. In

"The Banks of the Lee," composed to the air "A Trip to the Cottage," Davis adheres closely to the precepts of Wordsworth, whom he admired and appreciated. Davis pictures a happy couple living in tune with the changing seasons, a pastoral archetype:

> Oh! the banks of the Lee, the banks of the Lee,
> And love in a cottage for Mary and me;
> There's not in the land a lovelier tide,
> And I'm sure there's no one so fair as my bride.
>   She's modest and meek,
>   There's a down on her cheek
>   As a butterfly's wing—
> Then her step would scarce show
> On the fresh-fallen snow;
> And her whisper is low,
>   But as clear as the spring.
> Oh! the banks of the Lee, the banks of the Lee,
> And love in a cottage for Mary and me.
> I know not how love is happy elsewhere;
> I know not how any but lovers are there!

The pastoral image, possible in agricultural Ireland, was not a common scene, but it was Davis's dream and the dream of the readers of *The Nation*.

In "The Girl of Dunbury," Davis realistically sketches a beautiful young girl in a natural setting:

> Tis pretty to see the girl of Dunbury
> Stepping the mountain statelily;
> Though ragged her gown, and naked her feet,
> No lady in Ireland to match her is meet.
>
> Poor is her diet, and hardly she lies—
> Yet a monarch might kneel for a glance of her eyes;
> The child of a peasant—yet England's proud Queen
> Has less rank in her heart, and less grace in her mien.

The Wordsworthian quality is detected in these two stanzas of a six-stanza poem. By acknowledging the beauty and poverty of the girl of Dunbury, Davis gives a glimpse of country life. Many such girls stepped over mountain stones; however, Davis fantasizes when he tells us a monarch might kneel for a look into her eyes. Authority, fashion, and elegance fall before equality, rags, and simplicity! The effect of the poem is to exalt the poor, beautiful, passionate mountain girl at the expense of merry monarchs and proud queens. But a great leveler cannot praise the mighty Irish heroes, kings, and leaders on one plane because of their exceptional nature while condemning English heroes, kings, and leaders without incurring the charge of sentimentalism. And how many readers will permanently accept the loss of authority, fashion, and elegance for the simple stone-stepping girl who eats poorly but leads a moral life? Displeased by the image of a poorly fed farm girl in a beautiful natural scene, we are more apt to think man's depravity is out of phase with nature's design. The Dunbury girl is the archetype of the moral maid and contrasts with the cunning, self-centered, fashionable queen. But praising the idealized girl's superiority did not alleviate the real Irish girl's problems. In fact, were the latter persuaded to believe the fantasy of the poem, she might believe that moral superiority would protect her or offer social salvation in political turmoil, which it could not. To forge a nation and break the ties from England required much stronger women — such as Ireland historically provides — than Davis here eulogized. This type of poem, expressing the charm and morality of the country girl, has the opposite effect as a national poem from that intended, for it dulls the intellect for the great task of nation building.

Davis is more effective in his explicitly nationalistic and propagandistic poems. For these pieces he will long be remembered in Ireland after the girls of Dunbury are forgotten. In the nationalist poems he resembles his American contemporaries Longfellow, Cooper, and Lowell, who expressed a near-religious devotion to the ideal of national literature and believed that native writers could acquire literary fame.

Another similarity existed between Davis and the Americans; they shared the problem of writing in English without being part of the English culture. How could writers in English, subject to the restrictions of that language, develop a lively literature when its subject matter and dialect were designed to appeal to a non-English literary audience? Inevitably, too, both Irish and American writers would be evaluated by English tastes and standards. Such judgments would conceal more of the qualities of the native literature than they would reveal. Obviously, the Irishmen and the Americans were influenced by contemporary English writers: Davis was particularly influenced by Carlyle and Wordsworth. But when Davis and the Americans used Irish and American themes, they enriched the great body of literature written in English because their folk heroes were beyond the English tradition. Devotion to past native heroes and happenings became part of their conscious effort to create a national literature. For Davis, that meant that he would eulogize the Milesians, past Irish kings, the Geraldines, O'Sullivan Beare, Eoghan Ruadh O'Neill, Sarsfield, the Volunteers of 1782, Clare's Dragoons, the Dungannon Convention, the

Penal days, O'Connell, Tone, and the exiles. By dedication and education, and through his journalistic relationships, Davis created Irish literary pieces for *The Nation*. And he did so by studying Irish history and writing poems on all of the above-mentioned heroes as part of his contribution to the nation.

As Davis became more deeply involved in his public life, his academic training surfaced and served him well. Admitting that thoughts of a united Ireland haunted his mind, Davis wrote "Tone's Grave" to rekindle the flame that burst from Belfast in 1791 when Theobald Wolfe Tone founded the United Irishmen Society. Tone, like Davis, was a Protestant, a lawyer, a nationalist, and a believer in civil, political, and religious liberties for all Irishmen. Temporarily exiling himself to America and France, Tone returned to Ireland during the Revolution of 1798, was captured, and was sentenced to death. Mysteriously, his throat was slit while he awaited execution in a Dublin Jail, and he died from that wound. Davis wanted to pay homage and respect to the Irish hero. Finding Tone's grave unmarked and unvisited, Davis wrote "Tone's Grave," a lyrical tribute to a lost leader. There are eight stanzas; the first three and the last carry the poem's thematic burden:

> In Bodenstown churchyard there is a green grave,
> And wildly along it the winter winds rave;
> Small shelter, I ween, are the ruined walls there
> When the storm sweeps down on the plains of Kildare.
>
> Once I lay on that sod—it lies over Wolfe Tone—
> And thought how he perished in prison alone.
> His friends unavenged, and his country unfreed—
> "Oh bitter," I said, "is the patriot's need;

> For in him the heart of woman combined
> with a heroic life, and a governing mind—
> A martyr for Ireland—his grave has no stone—
> His name seldom named and his virtues unknown."

. . . .

> In Bodenstown churchyard there is a green grave,
> And freely around it let winter winds rave—
> Far better they suit him—the ruin and gloom—
> Till Ireland, a nation, can build him a tomb.

Both the nature of the poem and its desired effect were made manifest by a local response to the poem from the villagers in neighboring Clongowes. Justin H. McCarthy in *Ireland Since the Union* reports that the villagers placed an iron rail around the grave-site. A stone slab, recording the heroic deeds and ending with "God Save Ireland," was also placed on the grave. Davis's poem produced results and sparked a sense of local pride in Tone and the ill-fated Revolution of 1798.

"Native Swords" was written in a conscious attempt to revive memories of the daring deeds of the eighteenth century. This four-stanza song indicated the superiority of the sword over moral sanction when a patriot is trying to gain and maintain political freedom. The widespread popularity of this and other songs was an achievement that hardly anyone could measure—except, perhaps, for Charles Gavan Duffy and John Blake Dillon. They realized the immense appeal that the national songs had for the laboring millions, the native Irish. William Carleton, assuming the role of social historian, wrote *Traits and Stories of the Irish Peasantry* and *Valentine M'Clutchy, the Irish Agent* to dramatize the life of the farm workers. However, he was not politically oriented. Carleton described the class; Davis called it to battle. The first and last stanza of "Native Swords" carries that call to arms:

> We've bent too long to braggart wrong,
>   While force our prayers derided;
> We've fought too long ourselves among,
>   By knaves and priests divided.
> United now, no more we'll bow,
>   Foul faction we discard it;
> And now, thank God! our native sod
>   Has native swords to guard it.
>
> . . . .
>
> But now, no clan, nor factious plan,
>   The east and west can sunder—
> Why Ulster e'er should Munster fear,
>   Can only wake our wonder.
> Religion's crost, when union's lost,
>   And "royal gifts" retard it;
> But now, thank God' our native sod
>   Has native swords to guard it.

Davis wrote three songs to remind his countrymen of Grattan and the Volunteers, "Song of the Volunteers of 1782," "The Dungannon Convention," and "The Men of Eighty-Two." "Song of the Volunteers of 1782," like "Native Swords," was written to the tune of "The Boyne Water." The second of the five stanzas is another example of Davis's faith in the necessity of both words and weapons to assure civil liberty:

> When Grattan rose, none dared oppose
>   The claim he made for freedom:
> They knew our swords, to back his words
>   Were ready, did he need them.
> Then let us raise to Grattan's praise,

A proud and joyous anthem;
And wealth and grace and length of day,
May God, in mercy, grant him!

Here, Davis summons the men of Ireland to join the struggle for independence. He, and others like him, would be parliamentarians, but an army was necessary, too. The populace would have to be roused to supply the force. In Ireland's case, it was pikes and a small arsenal against an Empire because of the profound contrast between the aristocracy and the laboring class. The parliamentarians of 1843 lacked an armed populace because the citizenry had no right to bear arms. Still, Davis sounded the battle call, though it could not be answered by a force of 40,000 armed men to equal Grattan's volunteers.

Grattan, one of Davis's favorite heroes, was the type of national hero who could appeal to Protestant Irishmen in 1843. In his role of legend-maker for all Ireland, Davis had to resurrect just the proper Protestant, It would not do to honor Protestants disdained by native Catholics, and Davis avoided such a blunder. The moderate Protestants were elusive, gentle folk who disliked both O'Connell and England's control of their destiny. Their dislike of the latter could be intensified while diluting some of their distaste of the former by bringing Grattan's name before them. After all, he did tell the Volunteers, Anglican and Presbyterian, that "as Irishmen, Christians, and Protestants, we rejoice at the relaxation of the penal laws against our Roman Catholic fellow-subjects." Such sentiments had to be voiced over and over again to influence Protestant thought because the status of nationhood depended upon its intellectual commitment. That one commitment was crucial in 1843, as it was in 1782 when Grattan was trailblazing for Tone, Fitzgerlad, Emmet, and Davis himself. The purpose of the "Song of the Volunteers of 1782" was also partially educational. Davis wanted to show that, whether or not Protestants agreed with O'Connell, they had no choice but to work for his goal. Thomas Osborne Davis, hoping for their loyalty, aimed at simplicity, spirituality, and righteousness in his ballads to attract Protestants to his cause. Everyone has to answer for his conscience, Davis thought; therefore he would try to get at the collective Protestant conscience, which by its nature was a protest against wrong. The Dublin lawyer had not set out to invent anything in 1843; he simply wanted to make something right. Fellow Protestants, he appealed, look at the suffering around you. It is there, palpable and visible. Imitate Grattan.

Davis expected the Irish Protestants to abstract from that complex situation of 1843 some simple relationships that might guide them. Doing so, they would acquire a kinship with the majority of the inhabitants of the island, creating a real bond and sense of nationality. It had happened before, Davis knew, and it could happen again. In his praiseworthy bid for national kinship, Davis wrote "The Dungannon Convention, 1782."

Five stanzas express the usual theme: the need for arms to support civil rights. But another idea is presented for his fellow Protestants to think about: the role of their Church in nationalism. One thing Protestant nationalists had to worry about in 1782 was the possibility that Catholics would use their newly acquired civil rights to deny civil rights to Protestants

and threaten Protestant economic prosperity. The possibility of such an occurrence clearly depended upon the
vigor of anti-Protestant feelings and the enforcement of
such feelings. Catholics in the eighteenth century,
experiencing the workings of laws forbidding their
involvement in civic and economic affairs, might have
retaliated. However, men like Grattan did not feel
threatened. By analogy, Davis argued that in 1843 the
Church of Ireland and other Protestant churches could
foster nationalism without fear of reprisals. Any rights
granted to Catholics would not endanger their economic
status. It was safe for Protestants to participate in the
national movement because the Catholics were no
threat, and English oppression of trade nullified any
allegiance that Irish Protestants would have to Protestant Englishmen. The first and third stanzas of "The
Dungannon Convention, 1782" carried the theme of
armed resistance and church involvement:

> The church of Dungannon is full to the door,
> And sabre and spur clash at times on the floor,
> White helmet and shako are ranged all along
> Yet no book of devotion is seen in the throng.
> In front of the altar no minister stands,
> But the crimson-clad chief of these warrior bands;
>
> And though solemn the looks and the voices around,
> You'd listen in vain for a litany's sound.
> Say! what do they hear in the temple of prayer?
> Oh! why in the fold has the lion his lair?
>
> . . . .
>
> Oe'r the green hills of Ulster their banners are spread.
> The cities of Leinster resound to their tread,
> The valleys of Munster with ardour are stirred,

And the plains of wild Connaught their bugles have heard;
A Protestant front-rank and Catholic rere—
For—forbidden the arms of freemen to bear—
Yet foeman and friend are full sure if need be,
The slave for his country will stand by the free
By green flags supported, the orange flags wave
And the soldier half turns to unfetter the slave.

It becomes clearer with each poem that Davis believed Catholic and Protestant Irishmen would have to mobilize the necessary force to secure the change, if Ireland were to be politically free. When necessary, "the sabre and spur" must replace the "book of devotion." In truth, Davis thought clerical leadership would have to be suspended until political freedom was acquired. The ancient clan spirit with its militant chieftain could establish the just political system, and Davis calls for the Irishman of the old order from the Provinces of Ulster, Leinster, Munster, and Connaught to band together for the fight. He updates the factional symbolism in "The Dungannon Convention, 1782" to dramatize Ireland, 1843. Green and orange flags would be carried by unified Catholic and Protestant Irishmen.

To be sure, if the upper class would plan and execute social change, the process could evolve peacefully. In "The Men of 'Eighty-Two," a song with a lively beat, Davis pictures such an evolution. Composed to an Irish air "An Criúsgin Lán" (The Full Jug), seven stanzas of song praise the bishops, peasants, lords, traders, generals, soldiers, and sages working together for prosperity and peace. The second stanza of "The Men of 'Eighty-Two" depicts the various threads in Ireland's national robe:

Within that host were seen
The orange, blue, and green—

> The bishop for its coat left his lawn—
> The peasant and the lord
> Ranked in one accord,
> Like brothers at a criusgin, lán, lán, lán,
> Like brothers at a criusgin lán.

To attract the attention of Protestant moderates would not, however, be sufficient in the long run to build a nation where the majority of the population was Catholic. Davis was obliged to glorify the Catholic past and he honestly did so. "The Penal Days" sings the lamentations of the persecuted Catholics. Four stanzas outline the legislative cruelties inflicted upon Irish Catholics during the Hanoverian rule in Ireland. The second stanza of "The Penal Days" exposes the persecution:

> They bribed the flock, they bribed the son,
> To sell the priest and rob the sire;
> Their dogs were taught alike to run
> Upon the scent of wolf and friar.
> Among the poor,
> Or on the moor,
> Where hid the pious and the true—
> While traitor knave,
> And recreant slave,
> Had riches, rank, and retinue;
> And, exiled in those penal days,
> Our banners over Europe blaze.

In the third stanza Davis tells of the loss of "Popish lordly power," the poverty of the rural population, and the denial of legal rights, education, arms, and voting privileges to the Catholics. He concludes by joyously proclaiming the present situation:

> They're gone, they're gone, those penal days!
> All creeds are equal in our isle;

Then grant, Lord, Thy plenteous grace,
Our ancient feuds to reconcile.
Let all atone
For blood and groan,
For dark revenge and open wrong;
Let all unite
For Ireland's right
And drown our griefs in freedom's song,
Till time shall veil in twilight haze
The memory of those penal days.

Catholics could be moved by Davis's concern for their present plight and past terrors. "The Penal Days" sincerely expresses his desire to cement all factions into the house of Irish nationality. The nightmare of past history recognized, Thomas Davis wanted to construct a new edifice safe for all religious tenants. The secret of nationality, Davis thought, was in knowing how to keep the past in its place. He could not falsify historical happenings that he, as a Protestant, would have to condemn. Yet Davis had to discover the proper balance for the forces he sought to unite. Too much Catholic history could alienate his Protestant colleagues; too little Catholic history could offend his Catholic friends. In "The Penal Days" he manages to keep the balance by refusing to use the past to escape from the present but using it to put the present in perspective. Historically, Catholics had been barbarously abused by English law and order, and present agitation stems from past injustices. The song, however, ends on an optimistic note because the listener is carried through a century of tyranny to the present, when the penal years are to be only dimly recollected. Davis liked for the past to become the present and then become the past again.

To persuade his Catholic countrymen to his national-istic faith, Davis eulogizes their past leaders. Through the seventeenth century, Irish leaders had usually been Catholic and Irish speakers. One such seventeenth-century leader, well loved and respected, was Eoghan Ruadh O'Neill, who fought against the Cromwellian invasion in 1649. Though Davis on his mother's side was a descendant of a Cromwellian settler, looking back to the seventeenth century, he could see only the magnifi-cent O'Neill and composed the "Lament for the Death of Eoghan Ruadh O'Neill." As an elegiac exercise it is superb, one of Davis's most memorable poems. The last stanza is particularly moving:

> Soft as woman's was your voice, O'Neill!
>   bright was your eye,
> Oh! why did you leave us, Eoghan? Why
>   did you die?
> Your troubles are all over, you're at rest
>   with God on high,
> But we're slaves and we're orphans Eoghan! Why
>   did you die?

Owen Roe, "the Red" O'Neill, nephew of the great Hugh O'Neill, was a fine soldier who had a paid, well-fed, highly disciplined army. A statesman and persuader, he longed for a united Ireland. But the land was caught up in the convulsive movements of the English Civil War between the Puritans under Cromwell and the Cavaliers under King Charles I, and the battlefield was extended to Ireland. O'Neill's army had a decisive victory at Benburb in 1646, but there was no political structure to reap the harvest of battle. O'Neill died in 1649 and with him the leadership that could effect political autonomy.

Another seventeenth-century Catholic hero worthy of Davis's praise was Patrick Sarsfield. As Commander-in-Chief of the Irish forces at the Battle of the Boyne (1690), Sarsfield, representing the Catholic aristocracy, is a noble figure in Irish annals. He fought on in Ireland with French aid after James II left Ireland. Sarsfield surrendered to Williamite forces and signed the Treaty of Limerick, which was supposed to grant religious freedom to Catholics. He, along with 11,000 followers, sailed to France and entered her service as the Irish Brigade. Two years later he died from battle wounds suffered while fighting for King Louis, sighing "Oh! that this was for Ireland." Davis chooses Sarsfield's death to evoke an emotional response from his Catholic readers. "The Death of Sarsfield—A Chant of the Brigade" is a short poem of sixteen rousing lines. Sarsfield, the subject of each of four stanzas, in the final stanza is the model for Catholic patriotism, which was a long time returning to Ireland after his flight in 1691:

> Sarsfield is dead, yet no tears shed we,
> For he died in the arms of Victory,
> And his dying words shall edge the brand
> When we chaoo the fue from our native land!

It seems to me that Davis is also warning the young Dublin nationalists that military might, once assembled, should not be dismantled or beguiled by English political chicanery.

Other poems, "A Rally for Ireland," "The Battle Eve of the Brigade," and "The Battle of Limerick" were written to mark Catholic Ireland's struggle against William of Orange. In "A Rally for Ireland" Davis

pictures "Townsman and peasant like waves of the
sea—/ shoulder to shoulder for liberty." He saw the city
and country people united in their fight for freedom.
Davis, projecting the idea that liberty is possible for all
Irishmen, imagines armed Irishmen fighting for Ireland
rather than for other nations. In "The Battle Eve of the
Brigade" Davis describes the soldiers in the Irish Brigade
serving King Louis of France. They recollect past service
to James in Ireland, wishing, of course, that William had
been defeated. Still, while the Irish soldiers fight bravely
for the French cause, they miss Ireland: "But the land
of their heart's hope they never saw more." In "The
Battle of Limerick" Davis sings of Sarsfield's men to the
Irish air "Garradh Eoghain":

> . . . hurrah for the men who when danger is nigh
> Are found in the front, looking death in the eye!
> Hurrah for the men who kept Limerick's wall!
> And hurrah for bold Sarsfield, the bravest of all!

Brave men fighting for a just cause inspired Davis; he gave
literary and political value to their actions by drama-
tizing their deeds. Because seventeenth-century Irish
history enthralled Davis, he hoped that his literary
adaptations would inspire others to initiate a strong
national movement. By setting English words to Irish
airs, Davis combined two elements from the merging
cultures. Irish music, deeds, courage, and heroes were
preserved for the nineteenth-century Irish Catholic
majority that was in the process of losing its language
in the battle for economic survival.

Davis has also recorded the heroic lives of the
sixteenth-century Norman-Irish heroes of Gaelic Ireland,

when the Irish language was the language of its aristocrats, and Irish law ruled its various kingships. When in 1537, after almost two unhappy years in the London tower, Thomas, Lord Offaly was executed in England along with five of his Geraldine uncles, Henry VIII rid England of the Geraldine threat to his reign. In the third stanza of "The Geraldines," Davis combines their history with the idea of Irish invaders becoming Irish patriots— since at one time the Geraldines had been invaders. They conquered Ireland in the twelfth century and became "more Irish than the Irish."

These Geraldines! these Geraldines! not long our
air they breathed;
Not long they fed on venison, in Irish water seethed;
Not often had their children been by Irish mothers nursed;
When from their full and genial hearts an Irish feeling
burst!
The English monarchs strove in vain, by law, and force,
and bribe,
To win from Irish thoughts and ways this "more than Irish"
tribe;
For still they clung to fosterage, to breitheamh, cloak
and bard;
What king dare say to Geraldine, "Your Irish wife discard?"

If the Norman invaders were changed by the Irish countryside, could not Davis evoke in the hearts of his readers a psychic nationalism encompassing all racial stocks?

Davis often uses the word *dare* in writing about English oppression of Ireland. English presumption about the Irishman's lack of wisdom is so contrary to the fact that Davis wonders·how Englishmen can so often commit the offense. Since Davis himself knew

Irish history well, he knew the evolutionary process that Hibernicized invading armies; slow but effective, it turned victor to vanquished to victor again, because the victorious became part of the Irish culture, which in turn was subject to another invasion. Davis, playing his role, was part of the victor-vanquished cycle. Envisioning the old Irish aristocracy, Davis returned to prehistoric Ireland in the "Lament for the Milesians" who, according to tradition, invaded Ireland about the time of Alexander the Great, conquering the Tuatha De Dananh—a semi-divine race skilled in magic and the arts. To the air of "An bruach na carraige baine," he is again creating the "genius loci" to develop a sense of nationalism. Irish soil, stars, and sky must awaken those Irishmen with no allegiance to any of the organized national institutions. The first stanza of the "Lament for the Milesians" evokes a nostalgic feeling for the old chieftains who are now part of Irish ground and space:

> Oh! proud were the chieftains of green Inis-Fail;
>   As truagh gan oidhir 'n-a-bh-farradh!
> The stars of our sky, and the salt of our soil;
>   As truagh gan oidhir 'n-a-bh-farradh!
> (What a pity that there is no heir of their company)

Another part of the common heritage that Davis celebrated was the rich pagan past upon which St. Patrick in the fifth century built Irish Christianity. Rather sympathetic to King Dathi, the last pagan King to hold the high Kingship at Tara, Davis portrays Dathi's sudden death and its effect upon his followers. The historical poet also described in the twelve stanzas of "The Fate of King Dathi" the adventurous life of the pagan Irish on the verge of their religious conversion. The first stanza sets the scene:

> Darkly their glibs o'er hang,
> Sharp is their wolf-dog's fang,
> Bronze spear and falchion clang—
>   Brave men might shun them.
> Heavy the spoil they bear—
> Jewels and gold are there
> Hostages and maiden fair—
>   How have they won them?

The image of foot soldiers armed for battle with spears evokes a primitive past. To add appropriate sound to the antique picture, Davis uses the aaa b ccc b rhyme scheme, not unusual in Irish poetry, with the strongly accented initial syllables of each line. After the reader has envisioned an army with spoils, Davis asks the important question, "How have they won them?" The answer provided by the poem is no less important: by hand-to-hand combat.

Pagan Ireland, its Celtic myths and legends, was a common meeting ground for Anglo-Irish Protestants and Irish Catholics. Both groups could look back to that past for political traditions such as the selection of the king, the subject of "The True Irish King." Englishmen, "Sassanach serfs," can not give to their king such homage, devotion, and loyalty as Irishmen give to their monarch because Englishmen have little choice in the selection of the King:

> Yet not for his courage, his strength, or his name,
> Can he from the clansmen their fealty claim,

The poorest, and highest, choose freely today
The chief that tonight they'll as truly obey;
For loyalty springs from a people's consent,
And the knee that is forced had been better unbent.
The Sassanach serfs no such homage can bring
As the Irishmen's choice of a True Irish King!

Obviously, Irishmen should select their leader with national peace and prosperity in mind. In a poem entitled "Nationality," Davis goes further in depicting other aspects of nationhood. There were still so many factions and issues that split each faction that Davis in the first stanza persuades his readers spiritually, associating nationality with the transcendant quality of light and with godliness:

A Nation's voice, a Nation's voice,
    It is a solemn thing!
It bids the bondage-sick rejoice,
    Tis stronger than a king.
Tis like the light of many stars,
    The sound of many waves,
Which brightly look through prison bars,
    And sweetly sound in caves.
Yet it is noblest, Godliest known,
When righteous triumph swells its tone.

Integrity, freedom, and justice for all should be the goal of Irish patriots in establishing a nation. Davis hails these in the fourth and final stanza of "Nationality":

May Ireland's voice be ever heard
    Amid the world's applause!
And never be her flag-staff stirred,
    But in an honest cause!
May freedom be her very breath,
    Be justice ever dear,

> And never an ennobled death
>   May son of Ireland fear!
> So the Lord God will ever smile,
> With guardian grace upon our isle.

Clearly, then, nationality is a sacred entity, and the patriots are its high priests who must suffer and sacrifice for the establishment of a holy state. Societies in which the patriot-priest is associated with corruption, injustice, vulgarity, and banality lack nationality in the true sense. The same thoughts are verbalized in the song "Our Own Again":

> Calm as granite to our foes,
>   Stand for our own again,
> Till his wrath to madness grows,
>   Firm for our own again.
> Bravely hope and wisely wait,
> Toil, join, and educate;
> Man is master of his fate;
>   We'll enjoy our own again.

The commonplaces of traditional color symbolism were ready at hand for Davis to evoke nationalist feeling. In "Orange and Green Will Carry the Day," written to the tune of "The Protestant Boys," he pictures the end of factional feuds. However obvious the color associations, the third stanza is particularly moving, for it shows the horrible consequences of religious and political disunity:

> Fruitful our soil where honest men starve,
>   Empty the mart, and shipless the bay;
> Out of our want the oligarchs carve,

Foreigners fatten on our decay!
Disunited,
Therefore, blighted,
Ruined and rent by the Englishman's sway
Party and creed
For once have agreed—
Orange and green will carry the day!
Boyne's old water
Red with slaughter!
Now is as pure as an infant at play;
So in our souls,
Its history rolls,
And Orange and Green will carry the day!

Davis, in "The Green Above the Red" to the "Irish Molly O!" air, manages to combine his religious and nationalistic feelings to express a defiant, almost reckless, attitude toward England:

The jealous English tyrant now has banned the Irish green,
And forced us to conceal it like something foul and mean;
But yet, by heavens! he'll sooner raise his victims from the dead
Than force our hearts to leave the green, and cotton to the red. . . .
And, freely as we lift our hands, we vow our blood to shed
Once and for evermore to raise the green above the red.

Related to these poems of defiance and echoing Emerson's feelings, "Self-Reliant" transmits Davis's optimistic beliefs and self-understanding:

Though France, that gave your exiles bread,
Your priests a home, your hopes a station,
Or that young land where first was spread

The starry flag of liberation—
Should heed your wrongs some future day,
    And send your voice or sword to plead 'em,
With helpful love then help repay,
    But trust not even to them for freedom.
A nation freed by foreign aid
    Is but a corpse by wanton science
Convulsed like life, then flung to fade,
    The life itself is Self-Reliance.

It was the policy of *The Nation* to urge defiant, self-reliant, confident, courageous men to sue for their rights with a gun in one hand. Davis, while welcoming French and American aid to secure Ireland's independence, realizes that foreign help can not create a free nation. The population must be prepared for the political change and ready to accept the responsibilities of nationhood. Liberty bought by others' money and blood dies: it flourishes in a self-reliant populace.

When Daniel O'Connell and Charles Gavan Duffy were jailed on October 14, 1843, Davis did not give up, however heartbroken he was by the news of the arrests. To hold the splintered Repeal Association together, Davis wrote "We Must Not Fail." He sums up the status of nationhood in that poem, which is worth reprinting in its entirety:

We must not fail, we must not fail,
However fraud or force assail;
By honour, pride, and policy,
By Heaven itself—we must be free.

Time had already thinned our chain,
Time would have dulled our sense of pain;
By service long, and suppliance vile,
We might have won our owner's smile.

We spurned the thought, our prison burst,
And dared the despot to the worst;
Renewed the strife of centuries,
And flung our banner to the breeze.

We called the ends of earth to view
The gallant deeds we swore to do;
They knew us wronged, they knew us brave,
And all we ask they freely gave.

We took the starving peasant's mite
To aid in winning back his right,
We took the priceless trust of youth;
Their freedom must redeem our truth.

We promised loud, and boasted high,
"To break our country's chains, or die;"
And should we quail, that country's name
Will be the synonym of shame.

Earth is not deep enough to hide
The coward slave who shrinks aside;
Hell is not hot enough to scathe
The ruffian wretch who breaks his faith.

But—calm, my soul! we promised true
Her destined work our land shall do;
Thought, courage, patience will prevail.
We shall not fail!—we shall not fail.

Despite the eloquence of "We Must Not Fail," the national movement failed. The "starving peasant's mite" that supported O'Connell's political life had been spent in vain. A greater famine was ahead for the poor and starving population. Davis, weary and frustrated, continued to write for *The Nation,* trying to educate Irishmen of all creeds and class. Songs and ballads, the young lawyer thought, might do for Irish nationality what laws and briefs could not.

If the reputation of a song writer is established by the popularity of his songs and ballads, then Davis has stature as a nationalist poet, whatever his aesthetic limits. One song, "A Nation Once Again," is still sung in pubs in the Republic of Ireland and nationalist pubs in Northern Ireland. It is a spirited song that evokes nationalist feelings. The first of four stanzas recalls a young man's fervor:

> When boyhood's fire was in my blood,
>   I read of ancient freemen,
> For Greece and Rome who bravely stood,
>   Three hundred men and three men.
> And then I prayed I yet might see
>   Our fetters rent in twain,
> And Ireland, long a province, be
>   A nation once again.

As direct in its rhythm as in its theme, the heroic vision the stanza summons up can nevertheless explain how Thomas Davis— journalist, historian, political economist, romantic nationalist, song writer, essayist, and poet— could influence his contemporaries and ensuing generations. Men as different as John Mitchel and William Butler Yeats admired Davis's tenacity and tenderness. His short life, dedicated to public service and to national letters, is a model for nationalists struggling for independence, integrity, freedom, and justice.

Bibliography

Primary Sources

Davis, Thomas. *Essays Literary and Historical.* Dundalk: Dundalgan Press, 1914.
———. *Literary and Historical Essays.* Dublin: James Duffy, 1854.
———. *National and the Historical Ballads, Songs, and Poems.* Dublin: James Duffy, [1869?]
———. *National and other Poems.* Dublin: N. H. Gill and Son, 1907.
———. *The Patriot Parliament of 1689.* Dublin: Sealy, Bryers, and Walker, 1893.
———. *The Poems of Thomas Davis.* New York: P. M. Haverty, 1857.
———. *The Poems of Thomas Davis Now First Collected.* Dublin: James Duffy, 1846.
———. *Prose Writings.* London: W. Scott, [1890?].
———. *Selections from his Prose and Poetry.* Dublin: Talbot Press, [1914?].
Davis, Thomas, ed. *The Speeches of the Right Honorable John Philpot Curran.* Dublin: James Duffy, 1862.

Secondary Sources

Barry, Michael Joseph, ed. *The Songs of Ireland.* Dublin: James Duffy, 1849.
———. *The Songs of Ireland.* New York: Felix O'Rourke, 1873.
Carleton, William. *The Autobiography of William Carleton.* Introduction by Patrick Kavanagh. London, 1968.
———. *Valentine M'Clutchy, The Irish Agent.* 3 vols. Dublin, 1846.

Corkery, Daniel. "Davis and the National Language." In *Thomas Davis and Young Ireland*, pp. 14-23, Dublin: Government Publications, 1945.

Curtis, Edmund. *A History of Ireland*. London: Methuern and Co., 1968.

Duffy, Sir Charles Gavan. *Short Life of Thomas Davis, 1840-1846*. Dublin: Sealy, Bryers, and Walker, 1895.

―――. *Young Ireland*. London, 1880.

Fallon, Padraic. "The Poetry of Thomas Davis." In *Thomas Davis and Young Ireland*, pp. 24-27. Dublin: Government Publications, 1945.

Ferguson, Samuel. "Lament for Thomas Davis." In *Thomas Davis and Young Ireland*, p. 123. Dublin: Government Publications, 1945.

Gallagher, Frank. "Davis and the Modern Revolution." In *Thomas Davis and Young Ireland*, pp. 9-13. Dublin: Government Publications, 1945.

Griffin, Gerald. *The Poetical and Dramatic Works of Gerald Griffin*. Dublin: Jas. Duffy, 1874.

Griffith, Arthur, ed. *Thomas Davis: Thinker and Teacher*. Dublin: M. H. Gill, 1914.

Gwynn, Denis. *Daniel O'Connell*. Cork: Cork University Press, 1947.

―――. *Young Ireland and 1846*. Cork: Cork University Press, 1949.

Hone, Joseph. "Davis's Family and Social Life.' In *Thomas Davis and Young Ireland*, pp. 5-8. Dublin: Government Publications, 1945.

―――, ed. *The Love Story of Thomas Davis Told in the Letters of Annie Hutton*. Dublin: Cuala Press, 1945.

Lyons, F. S. L. *John Dillon, A Biography*. Chicago: University of Chicago Press, 1968.

Kellett, Lorna. " 'The Nation' in Mourning." In *Thomas Davis and Young Ireland*, pp. 32-37. Dublin: Government Publications, 1945.

MacDermott, Martin. *Songs and Ballads of Young Ireland*. London, 1896.

MacManus, Francis. "The Greatness of Thomas Davis." In

Thomas Davis and Young Ireland, pp. 1-4. Dublin: Government Publications, 1945.

MacManus, M. J. ed. *Thomas Davis and Young Ireland.* Dublin: Government Publications, 1945.

McCaffrey, Lawrence J. *Daniel O'Connell — the Repeal Year.* Lexington, Ky: University Press of Kentucky, 1966.

McCarthy, Justin H. *Ireland Since the Union.* London: Chatto and Windus, 1887.

McCay, Hedley. *Padraic Pearse: A New Biography.* Cork: Mercier Press, 1966.

Mitchel, John. *The History of Ireland.* Glasgow, 1869.

Moore, Thomas. *The History of Ireland.* 3 vols. London, 1835.

O'Donoghue, D. J., ed. *Essays, Literary and Historical by Thomas Davis.* Dundalk: Dandalgan Press, 1914.

O'Néill, Séamus. "Tomás Dáibhis-Staraidhe." In *Thomas Davis and Young Ireland,* pp. 114-15. Dublin: Government Publications, 1945.

Ó Súilleabháin, Tomás. "Thomas Osborne Davis, the Guiding Spirit of 'The Nation.' " In *The Young Irelanders,* pp. 26-36. Tralee: The Kerryman Ltd., 1944, 1945.

O'Sullivan, Donal. *Carolan, The Life, Times, and Music of an Irish Harper.* 2 vols. London: Routledge and Kegan Paul, 1958.

Quigley, Michael, ed. *Pictorial Record, Centenary of Thomas Davis and Young Ireland.* Dublin: Government Publications, 1945.

Rolleston, T. W., ed. *Prose Writings of Thomas Davis.* London: W. Scott, [1890].

———,Stopford, and Brooke, eds. *A Treasury of Irish Poetry in the English Tongue.* London, 1900.

Schiller, Johannes. *Thomas Osborne Davis, ein irischer Freiheitssänger.* Vienna and Leipzig: W. Braumuller, 1915; New York: Johnson Reprint, 1964.

Sheehy, Edward. "Davis's Social Doctrines." In *Thomas Davis and Young Ireland,* pp. 28-31. Dublin: Government Publications, 1945.

Yeats, W. B. *Tribute to Thomas Davis.* Cork: Cork University Press, 1947, 1965.

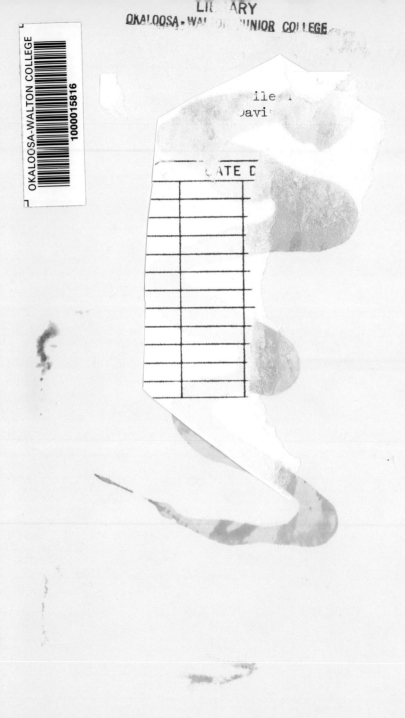

DATE D